This book will powerfully reinforce the truth that unrestricted evangelism is the product rather than the antithesis of Reformed theology. Without compromising on the doctrine of predestination, the reality of the human condition or the power of the Holy Spirit, Donald Macleod insists that Biblical evangelistic preaching must be directed to all, without qualification, and must be presented skilfully, passionately and persuasively. The gospel is a plea to the lost, sent out with a sincerity which originates in God Himself.

IVER MARTIN
Principal of Edinburgh Theological Seminary, Edinburgh

I first heard Donald Macleod preach nearly fifty years ago. As a teenager, I was blown away! I still remember the *richness* of that sermon. It was so biblical, so theological, so clear and so full of Christ. I also remember the *freeness* of the gospel offer that night, as the preacher threw himself into the most urgent and unequivocal offer of Christ to all.

The Professor's intellect and eloquence remain undimmed. This compelling new book proves we do not have to choose between distinctively Reformed theology and passionate evangelistic preaching. The universal offer is at the very heart of authentic Calvinism. Grace is rich and free.

ALASDAIR I. MACLEOD
Founding Pastor, St Andrews Free Church, St Andrews

Compel them to Come In isn't just for preachers. But it is for preachers. So allow me the liberty of addressing such directly. Is something holding you back from earnestly pleading with sinners to come to Christ? And if so, what is it? Is it the Bible's teaching on human inability? Or the doctrine of predestination? Or the conviction that Christ died only for the elect? Or the difficulty of believing that God actually desires all people to be saved? You need to read this book! For its purpose is to demonstrate that *nothing* should hold us back. Using both Scripture and the history of evangelistic preaching Donald Macleod deals with all the common obstacles that hinder Calvinists from passionately appealing to their hearers to believe in the Lord Jesus. And very effectively too. I found *Compel them to Come In* searching, humbling, convicting, encouraging, and deeply persuasive. In the hope that that's how *you* might find it, may I urge you to make time to read it?

DAVID CAMPBELL
Pastor, North Preston Evangelical Church, Preston, England

Too frequently the free offer of the gospel is hedged about with qualifications that distort the Biblical picture of the character of God and of Jesus Christ. This wonderfully clear book by a notable Reformed teacher and preacher will thrill the soul of any reader and encourage preachers to persuade sinners of every kind as they proclaim the Gospel to them.

ROWLAND S. WARD
Research Lecturer, Presbyterian Theological College, Melbourne

I always enjoy reading Donald MacLeod, as much for the clarity and precision of his arguments as for the elegance of his theology. Here he addresses an important topic – the free offer of the gospel – with his usual pungency and passion. It will clarify the issue for those who believe in the free offer but are confused by its connection to God's sovereignty; and it will hopefully persuade those who are tempted to truncate God's grace in a misguided attempt to exalt his election.

CARL R TRUEMAN
Professor of Biblical and Religious Studies, Grove City College,
Grove City, Pennsylvania

This is one of the most soul-stirring, liberating books that I have read on this subject. Donald MacLeod provides the reader with a necessary reminder to seek to persuade and implore men and women on Christ's behalf to be reconciled to God. I hope that it will show up in my preaching. I commend this book particularly to a rising group of young reformed pastors who when it comes to this matter of the 'free offer' are in danger of being tripped up by their own theological shoelaces.

Alistair Begg
Senior Pastor, Parkside Church, Chagrin Falls, Ohio

Compel Them to Come In is a wake-up call to the contemporary Church. We rejoice in multiple efforts to teach the Bible. Expository ministries abound and there is no want of edgy illustrations taken from the latest offerings from the silver screen or lyrics quoted from the current crooner of the moment. I may be wrong, but the impression left is that preachers may indeed present a message, but they exhibit a 'take it or leave it' attitude; there is a pervasive and soul-killing nonchalance in contemporary Bible teaching.

Donald Macleod was always the pastor-theologian but in all his ministries he did the work of an evangelist. Here we have an antidote to cool, professional detachment, as we are reminded that the business of evangelism is serious. There is a heaven to win and a hell to lose. Drawing from the wells of Scripture and the high-water marks of mission in Church history, we are reminded that the communication of the gospel must be carried out with passion, conviction and persuasion.

I hope that this book will provoke a discussion on the current state of preaching which is technically excellent but emotionally wanting. If the message of this book is not taken seriously, we are in danger of becoming functional Gnostics.

David C Meredith
Mission Director, Free Church of Scotland

Compel Him to Come In has all the trademarks we have come to recognise in Professor Donald Macleod's writings: mastery of doctrine, fulness of biblical insight, cogency of reasoning, clarity of expression, and an eloquence driven by the subject matter. At first you will think you are reading a powerful exposition of the free offer of the gospel in the face of criticisms and misunderstandings of reformed theology. It is indeed that. But by the end you will realise that it more. For *Compel Him to Come In* is really about the gospel itself. A book for all, it is a must-read for preachers, not least because it models the powerful, passionate appeals it commends.

SINCLAIR B. FERGUSON
Chancellor's Professor of Systematic Theology,
Reformed Theological Seminary, Jackson, Mississippi

COMPEL THEM TO COME IN

Calvinism and the
Free Offer of the Gospel

— ✝ —

DONALD MACLEOD

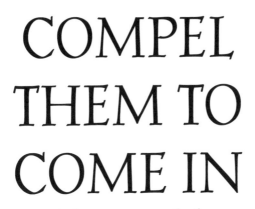

CHRISTIAN
FOCUS

Copyright © Donald Macleod 2020

hardback ISBN 978-1-5271-0524-9
epub ISBN 978-1-5271-0565-2
mobi ISBN 978-1-5271-0566-9

Published in 2020
by
Christian Focus Publications Ltd,
Geanies House, Fearn, Ross-shire
IV20 1TW, Scotland
www.christianfocus.com

Cover design by Rubner Durais

Printed and bound by Gutenberg Press Ltd, Malta

CONTENTS

Introduction

The most striking sermon I have ever read was preached by C. H. Spurgeon in the Music Hall, Surrey Gardens, on Sunday morning, 5th December, 1858.[1] The text was Luke 14:23, 'compel them to come in,'[2] and the preacher tells his congregation that he is in such haste to obey this command that he has no time for an introduction but must immediately set about his business; and he tells them, too, that he has nothing to say to the people of God this morning. He is going after those in the 'highways and hedges', those

---

1 See *The New Park Street Pulpit containing Sermons Preached and Revised by the Rev. C. H. Spurgeon During the Year 1859* (London: Passmore and Alabaster, 1884), pp. 17-24. Though the title refers to 1859, the first three sermons in the volume were preached in November and December 1858. The sermon is included as an appendix in this book.

2 Luke 14:23: 'And the lord said unto the servant, Go out into the highways and hedges, and compel them to come in, that my house may be filled' (KJV).

that will not come to Christ, and he must compel them to come in.

But, first, he must 'find' them, and he takes his cue from the context, 'Bring in hither the *poor,* and the *maimed,* and the *halt* and the *blind*' (Luke 14:21, KJV, italics added). As for the *poor*, their problem is not that they are poor in circumstances. They may well be, but that is no bar to the kingdom of heaven. His business is with those who are spiritually poor. They have no faith, no virtue, no good work, no grace and, worst of all, no hope. But he must lay hold of them and compel them to come in.

Then he speaks to the *maimed.* They have lost all power to save themselves. They feel they cannot believe, they cannot repent, or do anything pleasing to God. But to them, too, the preacher was sent, to lift up the blood-stained banner of the cross and declare, 'Who so calleth upon the name of the Lord shall be saved.'

Next to be addressed are the *halt*: halting, he says, between two opinions, sometimes savingly inclined, at other times called away by worldly gaiety. But the word of salvation is also sent to this limping brother: 'Halt no longer, but decide for God and His truth.'

And, finally, the *blind*, who cannot see their lost estate, or see that God is a just God, or see any beauty in Christ, or any happiness in religion: to them, too, he is sent.

But then, fearful that even after such a list he has not met every particular case, he notes that his text takes a general sweep, 'Go out into the highways and hedges.' Here, he says, 'we bring in all ranks and conditions of men – my lord upon his horse in the highway, and the woman trudging about her business, the thief waylaying the traveller – all these are in the highway, and they are all to be compelled to come in.' This is the universal command: 'compel them to come in.'

But no sooner has he said all this than he realises the herculean labour that lies before him: 'As well might a little child seek to compel a Samson, as I seek to lead a sinner to the cross of Christ. *And yet my Master has sent me about the errand*' (italics added).

And so he sets about 'the work', beginning with a survey of the great facts of the gospel ('what the King has done for you') before going on to direct a remarkable series of addresses to sinners. He *commands* them to repent and believe; he *exhorts* them to flee to Christ; he *entreats* them to stop and consider what they are rejecting; he *threatens* them with the prospect of a day when they shall no longer hear the voice of a gospel minister. This leaves only one more resort: he will *weep* for them. 'When words fail us,' he declares, 'we can give tears – for words and tears are the arms by which gospel ministers compel men to come in. You do not know, and I suppose could not believe, how anxious a man whom God has called to the ministry feels about his congregation.'

Even by Spurgeon's own standards this sermon was exceptional in its urgency, freeness and passion. Yet the message, and the tone of his message, was one that he maintained throughout his ministry. Sunday by Sunday, God in all His holiness, Christ in all His fulness, and gospel promises in all their glory, were pressed upon all within the reach of his voice. But inevitably such preaching had its critics, and Spurgeon was fully aware of them: 'Some hyper-Calvinist will tell me I am wrong in so doing. I cannot help it. I must do it. As I must stand before my Judge at last, I feel that I shall not make full proof of my ministry unless I entreat with many tears that ye would look unto Jesus Christ and receive his glorious salvation.' But such protestations were not enough to silence the critics. The preacher, they said, was betraying the Calvinism he professed to love. How could someone who believed in God's sovereign predestination offer Christ to sinners indiscriminately? How could someone who believed that human beings were by nature devoid of all spiritual ability nevertheless tell them it was their duty to believe in Christ? How could a man who knew that no one could come to Christ unless the Father drew him yet plead with them to look to the Saviour?

Today, there are still those who raise their voices against preachers who, they think, are too free with their evangelistic appeals; and, conversely, there are preachers who are inhibited in their evangelism by fear of such critics and by the feeling that they must always tread warily in relation to such doctrines as predestination and limited atonement. But the problem doesn't lie in these doctrines themselves. Men like Whitefield, Spurgeon and Chalmers believed in such doctrines as total depravity and unconditional election as firmly as any hyper-Calvinist; and they believed in them for the very good reason that they found them in Scripture. But they refused to follow the hyper-Calvinist in drawing from these doctrines inferences which Scripture itself never drew: the inference, for example, that since there was no universal redemption there should be no universal gospel offer. More important still, they refused to close their ears to the other voices they heard in Scripture, particularly the voices that commissioned them to bring the good news to every creature and to plead with sinners, simply as such, to be reconciled to God.

When Arminianism first appeared in Holland early in the seventeenth century some of the most distinguished divines in Europe gathered at the Synod of Dort (1618–19) to give an authoritative response on behalf of Reformed theology. The Synod spoke unambiguously of divine predestination, particular redemption and man's incapacity for any spiritual good. But, without a trace of embarrassment, the divines also went on to declare that 'the promise of the gospel, together with the command to repent and believe, ought to be declared and published to all nations, and to all persons promiscuously and without distinction, to whom God out of his good pleasure sends the gospel.'[3] It is to this, the indiscriminate preaching of the promise, and the universal call to repent and believe, that hyper-Calvinists raise their strong objections. Why?

---

3   *The Canons of the Synod of Dort*, Article II:V. See Philip Schaff, *The Creeds of the Evangelical Protestant Churches* (New York: Harper, 1882), p. 586.

1

The Free Offer and Man's Spiritual Bondage

The first objection raised against the free and indiscriminate offer of the gospel is that it implies that fallen human beings still have the capacity to repent and believe: a direct contradiction of St Paul's declaration that by nature we are all spiritually dead (Eph. 2:1), and thus totally incapable of any positive response to the gospel.

There can be no denying the fact. Paul states it again in 1 Corinthians 2:14: the 'natural' man *cannot* understand spiritual things, and because he cannot understand them he cannot accept them. To him the gospel, and especially the word of the cross (2 Cor. 1:18), comes across as 'foolishness'. It makes no sense. This is a note the Bible sounds repeatedly, and it is summed up in one of the most solemn paragraphs of the Westminster Confession (9:3) which lays down that man, by his fall into a state of sin, is completely unable, by his own strength, to convert himself, or even to prepare himself for conversion. His heart is closed against the gospel, he is a slave to unbelief, and completely blind to the beauty of Christ.

It is tempting to draw from this what looks like the cast-iron inference that there is no point in trying to persuade spiritually-dead men and women that it is their duty to repent and believe. The dead, after all, respond to no stimulus. They take no action, they make no decisions, and so any appeal to them is futile. Worse than that, urging them to believe confirms the delusion that they *can* believe and *can* repent and *can* turn to God at any moment of their own choosing. To put it in more philosophical terms, insisting that it is people's duty to believe seems to imply that they have the ability to believe.

Why then did the great Calvinist evangelists venture forth to the scattered hamlets and the great cities of Britain and America, and to the mission fields of India, Africa and China, to plead with all who heard them to turn to the living God? Did they not believe in the bondage of the human will? Of course they did! How then could they motivate themselves to such a futile action?

The short answer is, Because they took their cue not from human logic, but from the example of the Lord and His apostles, and accordingly saw it as their mission not only to proclaim the gospel but to persuade people to believe it.

Of course, proclamation mattered. Preachers are heralds, announcing a clear message. We see this in John the Baptist, proclaiming that the Kingdom of God is at hand. We see it in Jesus, proclaiming exactly the same message. We see it in the Apostle Paul, delivering the core Christian message that Christ died for our sins and rose again on the third day (1 Cor. 15:3-5). But they didn't simply announce. They pressed for a response, often reinforcing their pleas with the most solemn warning. 'Unless you repent,' declared Jesus, 'you too will all perish' (Luke 13:3). The language of the Great Commission (Matt. 28:18-20) likewise makes plain that Jesus intended His apostles (and their successors to 'the very end of the age') to be persuaders as well as proclaimers. Their preaching wasn't an end in itself. It had a clearly intended outcome: to enrol new converts in the school of Christ. There were to be joyful baptisms as well as faithful preaching.

The apostles carried out their commission with exemplary faithfulness, not only making sure that their hearers were fully informed as to what the Good news was, but urging them to repent and believe. We see this at the very beginning of the church's mission, the Day of Pentecost. Peter's sermon gives a full account of the life and ministry of Jesus, leading up to the great conclusion, 'God has made this Jesus, whom you crucified, both Lord and Christ' (Acts 2:36). It was a remarkable message, delivered with remarkable insight and power by the Spirit-filled Peter; and it called for a response. 'What shall we do?' cried the vast congregation. Peter had been long enough in his Master's company to know that without divine grace no one could accept Jesus as the Messiah. But he wasn't horrified by the word 'do'; nor does he tell them that all they can do is wait to be drawn. He commands them, every one of them, to repent; and he commands them to be baptised. Baptism was the easy bit. Anyone can volunteer to be immersed, sprinkled or dipped. But repentance is an inward thing, involving a revolution of the heart and the mind, and a whole new attitude to God. Many of those in Peter's audience had probably joined in the chant, 'Crucify! Crucify!' when Jesus had stood trial before Pilate; and even those who had not were 'dead in trespasses and sins'. How could they repent, and completely change the motives of their hearts and the direction of their lives? Yet that's what Peter commanded, 'Repent and be baptised, *every one of you*, in the name of Jesus Christ' (Acts 2:38, italics added); and that's what thousands of them did.

But Peter didn't merely command. He was addressing a vast concourse of people, some elect and some not elect, but he made a promise to one and all without distinction: if they repented and were baptised they would receive two amazing blessings: the forgiveness of their sins and the gift of the Holy Spirit (Acts 2:38). And still, like every preacher since, he found it difficult to bring his sermon to a close. He 'warned' them and he 'pleaded' with them, 'Save yourselves.' Yes! Save yourselves! That sermon, by the grace and power of God, persuaded over three thousand people to accept Jesus as the Messiah, and they were baptised without delay: a huge accretion to the number of believers (Acts 2:41).

But at the end of the chapter we find another remarkable touch. According to verse 40, the new believers had 'saved themselves'. In verse 47, however, we hear a different note: it is the Lord who adds to His church (Acts 2:47). We must never forget that. But neither may we forget that it was through Peter's forthrightness and persuasiveness that the Lord did it. As surely as the cross was a matter of God's determinate counsel and foreknowledge, so was the Apostle's sermon; but so too was the response of the three thousand. Without their repentance and faith there would have been no additions.

Here, at the very beginning of the New Testament age, we see that it was never enough for preachers merely to announce the good news. They had to press for a response, and in doing so they made clear that it was the duty of everyone who heard their message to believe it and to put their trust in Christ as the Saviour of the world. On this, the Apostle John leaves us in no doubt. 'This,' he writes, 'is [God's] command, to believe in the name of his Son, Jesus Christ' (1 John 3:23). Hyper-Calvinists deplore the preaching of what they call 'duty-faith', but this is exactly what John is preaching. The command to believe in Christ has the same force as the great commands of the Decalogue, including the command to love the Lord our God with all our hearts. That command is far beyond the capacity of people who are dead in trespasses and sins, but it is still a categorical divine imperative. So, too, is the command to believe in Christ, and the Christian preacher is bound to press it home with all the force at his command.

In line with this, in the very passage which speaks of the wonder of God's love, the Gospel of John warns in the most solemn terms of the gravity of wilful unbelief. God so loved the world that for it he gave his one and only Son (John 3:16). This is indeed, 'Love divine, all loves excelling,' and no response of ours could ever match it. Yet a response is required: not one that bears any comparison with what God has done, but a response nonetheless. We must believe in the Son, and it is to this faith that the promise is given that we shall not perish, but have eternal life. Very different, however, is the destiny of those who refuse to believe: 'whoever does not believe is condemned already, because he has not believed in the name of the only Son of God' (John 3:18, ESV). Then, to give the point even greater emphasis, John adds: 'Light has come into the world, but men love darkness instead of light because their deeds were evil' (John 3:19). The same note is struck in John 16:9:

when the Spirit convicts the world of *sin*, what he focuses on is precisely the sin of not believing in Christ.

We find another clear instance of an apostle calling for faith in Christ in Paul's words to the Philippian jailer, 'Believe in the Lord Jesus, and you will be saved' (Acts 16:31). What's fascinating here is that the Apostle responds without a moment's hesitation to the question, 'What must I do to be saved?' He doesn't balk at the word 'do', nor does he feel any need to enquire first of all into the spiritual condition of the jailer or to ascertain his fitness and readiness to be introduced to Christ. He doesn't know if this man has experienced an appropriate 'law-work' or whether his heart is truly broken and contrite. Nor does he know whether this man is elect. What he does know is that the man who stands trembling in front of him is, in all likelihood, a brutal ex-soldier without even a veneer of humanity or the least semblance of piety or the most elementary knowledge of the Bible. And he knows, too, that the jailer is by nature utterly impervious to the appeal of Jesus. Yet he gives the man an immediate and unequivocal answer, 'Believe in the Lord Jesus.'

We have to note, of course, that he did not simply say, 'Believe.' He said, 'Believe in the Lord Jesus,' and this is why the Apostle immediately proceeded to speak the word about the Lord to him. The order may strike us as peculiar. Logically, the command to believe should come after the message: here it comes before it, but only because it was the jailer's question that provided the conversation-starter. As far as any knowledge of Jesus was concerned, he was starting from scratch, but we can be sure that the 'word of the Lord' included all the great features of Paul's preaching: that Jesus was the Son of God, that He became man, that He performed mighty acts, that He died for our sins, that He had risen from the dead, and that He now sat enthroned in heaven; and then, to crown it all, the word of personal testimony: 'I saw him after he rose from the dead.'

It is in this Christ that the jailer comes to believe, and it is in this Christ, this living person, that Christian faith always puts its trust. Our faith, as James Packer points out, is not in the atonement but in the Lord Jesus Christ who made the atonement.[1] It is this Christ whom St Paul, without a moment's hesitation, presents as Saviour to a man he had never met before, of whose spiritual state he knew nothing, and of whose place in the counsels of eternity he knew even less. We are to be equally bold, presenting Christ at the door of every human soul.

PROMISE AS WELL AS SUMMONS

But not only are we to present this Christ to the whole world and summon the whole world to believe in Him. To our

---

1   J.I. Packer, *Evangelism and the Sovereignty of God* (London: Inter-Varsity Fellowship, 1961), p. 66.

summons we are to attach a promise: believe *and you will be saved*. It is a promise the preacher is authorised to make, but it is not the preacher's promise. It is God's promise, and it is to be given 'promiscuously and without distinction' to all who hear the gospel. There is, of course, an *if* – *if* you believe. But to those who obey the command to believe, the promise is absolute, whatever their background in riotous living, however deep the stain of their sin, however chilling their blasphemies, however cruel their persecution of His church, however they have led others into sin. They all have a categorical assurance: whoever *comes,* I will not in any circumstances drive away (John 6:37). As countless Reformed preachers have emphasised, 'None are excluded but those who exclude themselves.'

'COME TO ME, ALL WHO ARE WEARY AND BURDENED'

Probably the best-known of all the gospel calls is the Lord's invitation in Matthew 11:28: 'Come to me, all who are weary and burdened, and I will give you rest.' On the face of things, Jesus is here opening His arms to receive the whole world, and on that assumption His words have provided the text for many a sermon in which Christ and His salvation were offered fully and freely to every sinner without distinction. Some, however, have objected strongly to this practice, arguing that the invitation, far from being indiscriminate, is addressed only to those who are already labouring under a sense of sin and guilt, and restless till they find peace with God. Only to such does Christ say, 'Come.'

The first response to this must be that the phrase 'weary and burdened' is a perfectly apt description of the whole human race. 'You have made us for yourself,' said Augustine, 'and our heart is restless until it rests in you' (*Confessions,* I:1). Jesus portrays humanity as haunted by anxiety over what to eat, what to drink, and what to wear (Matt. 6:25); the writer to the Hebrews describes us as enslaved by the fear of death (Heb. 2:15); and Ecclesiastes sums up our existence in the words, 'Meaningless! Meaningless! Utterly meaningless!' (Eccles. 1:2). People get nothing but pain for all their toil, writes the Preacher (Eccles. 2:22); justice and rights are denied; the oppressed have no comforter (Eccles. 4:1); the righteous get what the wicked deserve, and the wicked get what the righteous deserve (Eccles. 8:14); and even the rich are not immune to care. Their abundance permits them no sleep (Eccles. 5:12).

This is the plight of humanity, 'born to trouble as surely as sparks fly upward' (Job 5:7); and it is to man simply as man that the Lord's words are addressed. This note is already struck in the Old Testament. In Proverbs 8:4, for example, Wisdom cries, 'To you, O men, I call out; I raise my voice to all mankind.' In Isaiah 45:22, we find the same universal appeal: 'Turn to me and be saved, all you ends of the earth.' These Old Testament voices are echoed in Acts 2:39, where

Peter assures his audience that the Lord's call and the Lord's promise are not only for those then gathered before him, or only for the Jews, but for all who are afar off.

This universalism of the divine call has deep theological roots. The most obvious of these is God's love for the world, and one of the most remarkable references to this is in Titus 3:4, where Paul traces our salvation back to the 'kindness and love of God our Saviour'. This is a familiar biblical theme, but what is unusual here is the word the Apostle uses for 'love'. It is the word *philanthrōpia*, the root of our English word 'philanthropy', and it bespeaks God's love for mankind simply as such. We should feel no embarrassment in speaking of God as the supreme philanthropist, or of Jesus as the incarnation of that philanthropy. Time and again we read that He was 'moved with compassion', and it is that compassion that shines forth in His invitation to the burdened and weary in Matthew 11:28, just as it shone through in that moment when He beheld the city of Jerusalem and wept over it (Luke 19:41) and in that other moment when He observed that the crowds were like sheep without a shepherd (Matt. 9:36). Great lover of humanity as He was, the sight of our misery moved Him to the quick, and He longed to give us rest.

But Jesus' love for humanity simply as humanity had yet another root. He had taken our nature, become one with us and entered fully into the human experience. Of course, there was a special bond between Him and the elect, but there was also a bond between Him and all whose human nature He shared. The burdened and weary were *His* people in a way that no other species could ever be, and He had entered fully into their experience. Apart from sin, nothing human was alien to Him, and that included not only the burdens and the sorrows and the injustices which were their lot, but the weakness they experienced in trying to deal with them (Heb. 4:15). He was both an insider participating fully in the human condition, and an outsider observing it with compassion. What was unique was that He brought not only compassion, but also the power to give relief. What is astonishing is that He can offer it to the whole world.

The second difficulty with the idea that Christ is to be offered only to awakened and convicted sinners is that it implies that we must have certain qualifications before we take it on ourselves to accept His invitation. It is as if we were being told that He is not the Saviour of sinners but only of burdened and weary sinners, and that therefore our first step must be, not to come to Him, but to prepare ourselves for coming by working our hearts up to the right level of contrition and remorse. This takes us perilously close to the position of mediaeval Catholicism, which taught that man by nature has the ability to prepare Himself for grace, and even that such preparation makes us worthy of grace. Paradoxically, no one is more discouraged by such teaching than convicted sinners themselves. The more we strive to become truly penitential the more we seem to fall short. To the heart-broken sinner, her heart is never broken enough, and certainly never so broken as to give her a right and title to divine grace.

It is precisely such people who are most likely to be discouraged, and even driven to near-despair, by any preaching that suggests that the invitation of Matthew 11:28 is only for broken, convicted, and seeking sinners. This is why Hugh Binning, in a splendid sermon on this text, made plain his impatience with those who regarded Jesus' words as restrictive and exclusive, as if His reference to burdened and wearied sinners was a limitation of the command to believe, circumscribed the warrant to come to Christ, and debarred all who are not properly qualified. This, declares Binning, is 'contrary to the whole strain and current of the dispensation of the gospel'.[2] Christ meant to cast away impediments, not to cast delays in our way, and it was precisely to those who felt excluded that He addressed Himself: the 'babes', who saw themselves as so weak in understanding compared to the scribes; the weary and heavy-laden, falling so far short, as they saw it, of the righteousness of the Pharisees (or the glowing piety of real Christians). Such people will never

---

2   *The Works of the Rev. Hugh Binning*, ed. M. Leishman (1858. Reprinted Ligonier, PA: Soli Deo Gloria Publications, 1992), p. 579.

find peace by trying to bring their hearts to some deeper humiliation and delaying their coming to Christ till they have achieved it. They will find rest only in 'quiet yielding' to Christ's gracious offers because His is the only back that can take the burden of our sin and carry it away from us.

In sum, grace, to be grace, must be rich and free, which means it is never a response to anything remotely praiseworthy in ourselves. On the contrary, we come to Christ 'without one plea'; or, as it's put in Isaiah 55:1, the feast is for those who have no money. It's certainly hard to imagine any of us presenting ourselves before God pleading, 'Lord, be merciful to me the awakened and convicted sinner.' On the contrary, everyone who ever came to Christ will solemnly endorse the sentiments of Toplady's great hymn, 'Rock of ages':

> Not the labour of my hands
> Can fulfil thy law's demands;
> Could my zeal no respite know
> Could my tears for ever flow
> All for sin could not atone;
> Thou must save, and thou alone.

And this leads inexorably to the conclusion,

> Nothing in my hand I bring,
> Simply to thy cross I cling.

This was precisely the point of the Parable of the Great Banquet (Luke 14:15-24), from which Spurgeon took the text of the sermon with which we began. The master who sent out his servant to compel people to come to his feast didn't tell him to look out for people whom it would be an honour for him to entertain. In fact, the master's peers would have looked with disdain at the quality of his guests: the poor, the halt, the maimed and the blind. In the same way, the Christian preacher is not sent to scour the streets and alleys of the town looking for those already well on the road to spiritual recovery. He is sent to look for the spiritually poor and the spiritually blind, with the strict instruction that he is to compel them to come to the feast. Like the Lord Himself, his mission is to seek and save the *lost* (Luke 19:10).

Any remaining doubt on this score is dispelled by the Lord's letter to the church of Laodicea (Rev. 3:14-22). Here was a group of people who had no sense of spiritual need. Instead, they were complacent in the extreme, convinced they were in possession of such spiritual wealth that they needed nothing. They certainly had no idea that their lukewarm commitment was so offensive that the Lord would have been perfectly justified in spitting them out of His mouth. Yet, the Lord doesn't wait till these comfortable sinners become convicted sinners. Instead, He declares: 'I counsel you to buy from me gold refined in the fire, so that you can become rich; and white clothes to wear, so that you can cover your shameful nakedness; and salve to put on your eyes, so that you can see' (Rev. 3:18). With such an example before us, we have no right to hold back the gospel until we are sure that our hearers have a deep and genuine sense of spiritual need. Nor do those hearers themselves have a right to reject the Lord's counsel on the ground that His message is only for those who are deeply convicted and spiritually hungry.

FAITH BORN OF A SENSE OF NEED

Yet although conviction of sin and a sense of spiritual hunger are not qualifications that entitle us to a welcome from Christ, it is still true at the psychological level that without some sense of spiritual need no one will ever come to Christ. Hugh Binning clearly recognised this: 'though all ought to come to Christ, yet none will actually and really come till they are sensible of the weight of their sins, and the wrath of God.'[3] But Binning was merely repeating a point already made by the Lord Himself when he declared that 'Those who are well have no need of a physician, but those who are sick' (Matt. 9:12, ESV); and He repeated it moments later: 'I came not to call the righteous, but sinners' (v. 13). These remarks arose from the different attitudes to Jesus of tax collectors and sinners on the one hand, and the Pharisees on the other. The one group knew they were sinners; the other thought themselves righteous. The point is not that only

---

3   Hugh Binning, *Ibid.*

those who know they are sick *may* go to the Physician, but that only those who know they are sick *will* go to Him. The same principle is illustrated in the story of the Prodigal Son. The father would have welcomed him home at any point, but he actually went home only when he came to himself and saw the depths to which he had sunk.

It would be completely wrong, however, to conclude from this that preachers are to do nothing till the Lord Himself awakens the sinner and makes him a sin-sick soul. There has been a lack of balance here. In response to hyper-Calvinism we have tended to put all our emphasis on the freeness of the gospel and on the duty of offering Christ to all without distinction; and in doing so we could claim that we were acting in accordance with the instructions of the Synod of Dort. But have we given equal weight to Dort's other emphasis, namely, that the duty of *repentance* is also to be preached 'to all persons indiscriminately and without distinction'? Human beings, dead in trespasses and sins, are by nature as incapable of repentance as they are of faith. But the divine command is clear. We are heralds of both the command to believe and the command to repent, and this means that we are no more warranted in standing by and leaving it to God to awaken sinners than we are warranted in standing by and leaving it to God to give them faith. We have to awaken sinners. We have to create the sense of need without which they will never come to Christ. We have to face them with the truth about themselves.

This is yet another lesson from the Letter to the church of Laodicea. They thought they had need of nothing, but far from leaving them in their complacency the 'faithful and true witness' told them plainly that they were 'wretched, pitiful, poor, blind and naked' (Rev. 3:17). The same duty of plain speaking devolves on the modern Christian preacher. Far from waiting for sovereign grace or some special providence to awaken the sleeping souls in front of him, he has to engage in an awakening ministry. He knows full well, of course, that conviction of sin, and the creation of a broken and contrite heart, is something that in the last analysis only God the Holy Spirit can accomplish; and sometimes, as in the case of the Philippian Jailer, He does it without any human agency. He sends an earthquake. But His usual way is to awaken sinners through His Word, and the more we are convinced that only those who know they are sinners will come to Christ, the harder we will strive to convince our hearers that 'sinners' is exactly what they are, and that without forgiveness and cleansing their souls are in mortal peril. If it is only the smitten conscience that will seek peace through Christ, then the preacher must smite the conscience.

This is what the old divines spoke of as a 'law-work', but the most probing and searching of all preachers was the Lord

Jesus Christ Himself. He placed our lives in the full glare of the Law when He declared that unless our righteousness exceeds that of the scribes and Pharisees we shall never enter the kingdom of heaven (Matt. 5:20). He made plain that the real test of discipleship is whether we love God with all our heart. He laid down that love of neighbour includes love of enemy, condemned anger as well as murder, and lust as well as adultery. And He also warned, in the clearest possible terms, that sin had the most solemn consequences for our eternal destiny. There was, He said, a coming Day of Judgment when the sheep would be separated from the goats, and the latter hear the dread sentence, 'Depart from me, you who are cursed, into the eternal fire prepared for the devil and his angels' (Matt. 25:41).

The point bears repeating, then: the more we believe that only awakened sinners will seek a Saviour, the more we should strive to awaken them, and the more these solemn notes from the ministry of Jesus will feature in our preaching. We need to be as free with the call to repentance as with the call to faith. It is simply not good enough to say, 'Only those who are awakened will come,' and then sit back in pious inertia, comforting each other with the platitude, 'There's nothing we can do.' We can do what Jesus did, and the apostles did, and Jonathan Edwards did, and Robert Murray McCheyne did, and William Chalmers Burns did: speak plainly of sin and of a day of wrath, and plead with our hearers to make their peace with God. What we cannot do is to indulge in holy reveries while we wait for a stirring of the waters.

STEREOTYPICAL CONVERSION-NARRATIVES

But may such preaching not lead our hearers into the Slough of Despond? Yes, and at some time or other, and to some degree or other, every believer will find themselves in it. What is not warranted, however, is to insist that a period of intense conviction of sin is the invariable first step in a stereotypical conversion-narrative. It is indeed true that men like Martin Luther and John Bunyan went through prolonged periods of spiritual agony before they discovered the wonder of divine mercy and grace, and many personal Evangelical testimonies have recounted the same narrative of a journey to peace through near-despair: so much so, indeed, that those with a different story to tell have often been plagued with doubts as to whether they had ever been converted at all. Ministering to such people then became a serious pastoral challenge.

Yet such a stereotype can claim no warrant from the New Testament. Many New Testament figures became disciples of Christ without first having to go through a Bunyan-like experience. John the Baptist is one example, Matthew another (Matt. 9:9). Philip's experience was similar (John 1:43), and he in turn found Nathanael. In Lydia's case (Acts 16:14), the

Lord gently opened her heart. In other instances, no sooner is the soul convicted of its need than the need is met. The Philippian Jailer, for example, seems to find peace within minutes of crying out in fear, 'What must I do to be saved?' Many similar stories are told in accounts of revivals.[4] For others, however, the deepest pangs of contrition come not at the beginning of their spiritual pilgrimage but towards its close. David is a clear example. It was as a mature believer, and probably long after he had composed many of his immortal psalms, that he discovered the real depth of his own sinfulness; and pastors will have met many such cases.

None of this takes away from the fact that every believer is also by definition a penitent, but we have to bear in mind that the repentance of a new convert is the repentance of a spiritual child, and like every other grace it has to grow. This doesn't mean that as the Christian matures she sinks further and further into the Slough of Despond. On the contrary, our very immaturity may be the reason why 'darkness without light' marks the beginnings of many conversions. Our view of God may be radically unbiblical, as was that of Luther, who saw God as a terrifying figure who demanded righteousness rather than as one who gives

---

4   For example, in his account of the revival in Kilsyth in 1742, the minister, James Robe noted that some 'had the discovery of the remedy as soon as the misery' (*A Short Narrative of the Extraordinary Work at Kilsyth;* 1742. Reprinted as *When the Wind Blows*, Belfast: Ambassador Publications, 1985, p. 91).

it through faith. Or it may be that we have not yet reached the cross, and seen that the blood of Christ cleanses from all sin. Or our repentance may be profoundly influenced by the conversion-patterns we see around us, often as varied and distinctive as the theology and forms of worship of the church we belong to. It will also be affected by our personal temperaments, as it certainly was in the case of Luther and Bunyan, both of whom were depressives, and who would have experienced periods of severe mental darkness even if they had never been converted. Their clinical condition affected the spiritual part of their lives as it affected every other part.

No REPENTANCE APART FROM FAITH

But while the forgiven sinner is always a penitent sinner it is no less true that there can be no repentance apart from faith. The 'terrors of law and of God' may well fill us with fear, but they will never by themselves drive us to the throne of grace. Evangelical repentance, as the very name implies, has the gospel (the *evangel*) at its heart; or, as the Shorter Catechism (Answer 87) puts it, the penitent turns to God not only out of a true sense of his own sin, but also out of an 'apprehension of the mercy of God in Christ'. So long as we see God only as an angry judge who will throw the book at the sinner, we will never turn to Him. We must have hope: the sort of hope David had when he pled for forgiveness on the basis of the mercy and the love and the compassion of God (Ps. 51:1). We see the same thing again in the story of the Prodigal Son. He would never have ventured home if he thought he would be utterly rejected. Even though he misjudged his father's love, and could hope to be accepted only as a hired servant, it was enough to make him rise and head home.

In the *Marrow of Modern Divinity*, Nomista (the Legalist) argued that Christ requires true repentance *before* we can come to Him through faith. Evangelista argued the contrary: true repentance was impossible without faith.[5] This was exactly the position of John Calvin, who had declared not only that repentance always follows faith, but that it is produced by it (*Inst.* III:III, 1). This is why in the Scriptures the call to repentance is so often linked to the assurance of mercy. For example, when Isaiah urges Judah to come and reason together with the Lord (Isa. 1:18) he bases his plea on the hope that though their sins be like scarlet they would be as white as snow; and when, towards the end of his prophecy (Isa. 55:7), he entreats them to turn to the Lord, he bases his entreaty on the assurance that he will have mercy on them, and freely pardon. Jesus Himself encourages us to come to Him by assuring us that if we come we will not in

---

5   Edward Fisher, *The Marrow of Modern Divinity* (1645. New Edition with Notes by Thomas Boston, 1726. Reprinted New York, Westminster Publishing House, no date), pp. 142–50.

any circumstances be driven away (John 6:37). The Beloved Disciple encourages us to confess our sins by assuring us that if we do so, then God will forgive them and purify us from all unrighteousness (1 John 1:9); and to our endemic tendency to think of God as a punctilious tyrant he presents the wonder of the love which found expression on the cross of Calvary (1 John 4:10).

How careful the preacher must be here! He mustn't fall into the trap of imagining that he must postpone preaching the good news till he has first of all secured repentance through the preaching of the Law. Without the good news that 'this man receives sinners', and that God's throne is a 'throne of grace', no stricken conscience is ever going to leave the Far Country and venture anywhere near the Holy. But the preacher must also avoid conveying the impression that God's love is conditional on our faith and repentance. God did not send us into the world with the commission: 'Tell them that if they believe in me, then I will love them.' He has sent us to present to the world the love that bore the world's sin on the cross of Calvary, to expound it in all its Christ-centred glory, and to persuade the world to believe in it. And He has sent us to assure everyone who hears us that, precisely because they belong to the world, this love is for them. It is incarnate in Christ, and in Him it says, 'Come!'

2

The Free Offer and the Doctrine of Predestination

It is not only the doctrine of man's spiritual deadness that has been used to condemn the practice of pressing God's offer of salvation on every sinner. The same inference has been drawn, probably even more frequently, from the doctrine of predestination. Here again, however, the difference in practice between hyper-Calvinists and men like C. H. Spurgeon cannot be put down to a difference in doctrine. Spurgeon, as we have seen, believed with all his heart that from all eternity God had set His love on His elect and predestined them to be called, justified and glorified (Rom. 8:30); and the same was true of such soul-winners as Jonathan Edwards, George Whitefield, William Chalmers Burns and the countless other missionaries and evangelists who went forth from the Reformed churches inspired by the theology of the Westminster Confession.

WE ARE COMMANDED TO BRING THE GOSPEL TO THE WHOLE HUMAN RACE

Surely the first point to be made here is that the greater our respect for the sovereignty of God the greater should be our alacrity in responding to Jesus' imperious command, 'Go and make disciples of all nations': a command based on an unambiguous statement of the universal dominion of Christ, 'All authority in heaven and on earth has been given to me' (Matt. 28:18). It would be daring in the extreme to countermand such a charge by protesting, 'But, Lord, if they are elect they will be saved whether we evangelise them or not; and if they are not elect, they will not be converted no matter how earnestly we evangelise them.' The command stands, and its scope is universal: 'Go and make disciples of all nations.' This echoes God's promise to Abraham, 'In your seed will all the nations of the earth be blessed,' and it marks a key moment in the history of redemption. No longer are the great covenant promises to be confined to Israel, Abraham's physical seed. They are now to be extended to the Gentiles, and to them simply as Gentiles. By divine command, the gospel is to be taken to all those nations which have hitherto lived in spiritual darkness (Acts 26:18). Nor should this have come as a surprise to the disciples. Even before His crucifixion Jesus had made plain, when defending the woman who had poured an expensive perfume over His body, that the gospel was to be preached throughout the world (Matt. 26:13); and in the teaching He had given the apostles between His resurrection and His ascension He had given clear instructions that they were to carry their witness to Him to the ends of the earth (Acts 1:8). This is precisely the vision encapsulated in the Lausanne Covenant (1974): 'World evangelisation requires the whole Church to take the whole gospel to the whole world.'

It is a daunting task. It is not, however, one we face alone: 'I am with you always, to the very end of the age' (Matt. 28:20). One implication of these words is that the Great Commission was not given to the apostles alone, but to the church of all ages; and whether we live in an age of spiritual revival or an age of spiritual declension, the promise stands: Christ goes with us. But another implication is that the church which does not 'go', and which has no interest either in bearing witness to Christ in its own local culture or in sending the gospel to the 'ends of the earth', must seriously question whether it has any title to the promise of His presence. Christ is with us only in our going, and when we do go, we have the further encouragement that we can never, anywhere, find ourselves in a part of the world where we are not under His jurisdiction and encouragement. Wherever the sun rises and sets, Christ is Lord and is always there before us.

GOD'S OWN CALLS ARE ADDRESSED TO MEN INDISCRIMINATELY

The second point to note with regard to the connection between the gospel call and the doctrine of predestination is that the Bible records countless instances where God's own personal calls are addressed, not to the elect, but to the whole human race. Sometimes the call is to the ends of the earth, as in Isaiah 45:22, where God pleads, 'Turn to me and be saved, all you ends of the earth'; sometimes to men simply as men, as in Proverbs 8:4, where Wisdom cries, 'To you, O men, I call out; I raise my voice to all mankind'; and sometimes to 'the wicked', as in Isaiah 55:7: 'Let the wicked forsake his way and the evil man his thoughts. Let him turn to the Lord, and he will have mercy on him, and to our God, for he will freely pardon.' And even when God's call is directed specifically to Israel, it is not addressed to the faithful remnant (the elect), but to ethnic Israel as a whole. 'Turn! Turn from your evil ways!' cries Ezekiel, 'Why will you die, O house of Israel?' Similarly, it is to rebellious and impenitent Israel that God makes His appeal in Isaiah 1:18: '"Come now, let us reason together," says the Lord. "Though your sins are like scarlet, they shall be white as snow."'

The Christian preacher, as God's agent, is surely warranted to take his cue from such divine calls, addressed indiscriminately to the whole human race. This is certainly what we hear in Peter's sermon on the Day of Pentecost. He

urges his hearers to repent and be baptised, he promises that
if they do so they will receive the gift of the Holy Spirit, and
he backs this up with the assurance, 'The promise is for you
and your children and for all who are far off' (Acts 2:38-
39). His message had a powerful impact: three thousand
were added to the infant church, but impressive though the
figure is, it was but a proportion of the vast gathering. The
plea and promise were addressed to all, but even on such a
memorable day it fell on many deaf ears. Not all who were
privileged to hear, were elect; not all believed; and many of
them probably never heard the gospel again.

We find the same pattern in the ministry of Jesus. While
it was largely confined to His own people (John 1:11) it
embraced both those who received Him and those who did
not; and in line with this He made plain, in the Parable of the
Sower, that the good seed was to be sown indiscriminately,
falling on stony ground as well as on good ground;
sometimes bearing an abundance of fruit, and sometimes
none (Mark 4:1-20). That is a risk that all preachers must
take. The Parable of the Dragnet (Matt. 13:47-50) makes
the same point: the 'fishers of men' are to cast their nets at
random, with the inevitable result that they gather fish of
every kind, some so bad it has to be thrown away. Those
inclined to be critical of great spiritual movements on the
ground that some, or even many, of the 'converts' fell away
should bear this in mind. It was as true of the ministry of the

apostles as it was of George Whitefield and Billy Graham. But neither the risk of apostasy nor the fear of the message being despised should deter us from preaching it. The Lord Himself constantly exposed Himself to the risk of being rejected, and sometimes it wasn't just a risk but a painful reality. One such rejection is clearly recorded in John 6:60–66. Jesus had just performed one of His greatest miracles, the Feeding of the Five Thousand, and the following day, confronted by a great crowd, He had proclaimed Himself the Bread of Life and promised that those who come to Him will never hunger. Yet few of His hearers believed Him. Instead, many of those who had previously been following Him 'turned back' (John 6:66).

These are important lessons not only for those inclined to pass censorious judgment on other people's approach to evangelism, but for all missionaries and evangelists. As Jim Packer points out, there is no magic even in theologically impeccable messages or in theologically impeccable methods.[1] But neither, on the other hand, should our apparent failure rush us into changing our message, far less into replacing the preaching of the Word with something else. The most diligent, prayerful and wisest missionary may toil for long and see no fruit. The Lord Himself had the same bitter experience.

---

1   J. I. Packer, *Evangelism and the Sovereignty of God*, p. 117.

THE DOCTRINE OF PREDESTINATION: AN INCENTIVE TO EVANGELISM

Thirdly, the doctrines of election and predestination, far from being a disincentive to evangelism, are in fact our greatest encouragement. We see this clearly in Luke's account of Paul's ministry in Corinth. It was no easy assignment, and the Apostle, having been opposed and abused, was clearly in need of encouragement. It came when the Lord spoke to him in a night-time vision. 'Do not be afraid,' He said, 'keep on speaking, do not be silent. For I am with you, and no-one is going to attack and harm you, *because I have many people in this city*' (Acts 18:9-10; italics added). This echoes the words of Jesus Himself in John 10:16: 'I have other sheep that are not of this sheep pen. I must bring them also. They too will listen to my voice, and there shall be one flock and one shepherd.'

On the face of things, evangelism is a hopeless, even an absurd undertaking. We are confronted not only by apathy but by deep-rooted hostility; and not only by hostility but by a constitutional inability on the part of ordinary men and women to understand what we are saying (1 Cor. 2:14). The cross is offensive, the resurrection incredible, the cost of discipleship often fatal to the plans people have for their own lives. But what Paul was told in the vision was that among such people there were men and women whom God had 'had' from all eternity, which meant, in effect, that his commission, and the commission of all evangelists, was to gather God's elect. Many of those elect, like Paul himself, would be most unlikely subjects of God's mercy, but when the full tale was told, they would be a multitude too great to count (Rev. 7:9). Whatever sphere we labour in, then, and whatever gathering we address, this must be our hope and encouragement (always bearing in mind that conversions are seldom the result of a single sermon). We are about God's work and there is always good reason to hope that if God has sent us here it is because in this particular audience there are those whom He has ordained to eternal life and whom He is now calling through His Word.

THE ELECT CANNOT BE SAVED UNLESS THEY HEAR THE GOSPEL

But alongside this we must set another fact: the elect cannot be saved unless they hear the gospel. 'Who,' asks Augustine, 'calls upon you when he does not know you?' (*Confessions* 1.1). St Paul makes the point forcibly in Romans 10:13-15: it is those who call on the name of the Lord who will be saved, but how, he asks, can they call on one they have not believed in? How can they believe in one of whom they have never heard? How can they hear of Him unless someone preaches to them? And how can they preach unless they are sent?

The underlying premise is clear: faith and repentance both depend on information, and it is the business of the preacher to supply it. This doesn't detract from the fact that both these graces are God's gift, but God gives them through human agency, and specifically through the preaching of the gospel. His Word places our sins and shortcomings in the light of His holiness and justice, but at the same time it points us to the gospel of forgiveness: God has laid on Christ the iniquity of us all (Isa. 53:6). For the believer, this is a *eureka* moment. 'If you, O Lord,' cries the psalmist, 'kept a record of sins, who could stand?' But then he immediately adds, 'But with you there is forgiveness!' (Ps. 130:3-4). How does he know? Because of a divine word: 'in his word I put my hope.' Conscience can convict us of sin and subject us to agonies of remorse; only God's word of forgiveness can give us hope, and it is the duty of the preacher to deliver it. This is what makes mission and evangelism imperative. No one can believe in a Christ of whom they have never heard, and it was because he felt this so keenly that St Paul devoted his life to preaching the gospel where Christ was not known (Rom. 15:20). Only through such preaching, addressed to the whole world, can the elect be reached.

But the preacher is not merely a bearer of information. He must go beyond that. He must convince and persuade. He looks for conversions and baptisms (Matt. 28:19). He yearns to see men and women introduced to the Lord Jesus

Christ and bound to Him for time and eternity. 'Wherever this gospel is preached,' wrote James Durham, 'there Christ is laid, as it were, at the feet and door of every soul that heareth it, to be believed and rested on.'[2] There could be no better description of the gospel offer Christ laid at the sinner's feet, 'so near they have no more to do but consent to the bargain.'[3] We don't have two separate forms of the gospel, one for the elect and one for the reprobate. We have one gospel, with one very specific address: 'To sinners.' And by the same token it is the fact that he is a sinner, not the fact that he is elect, that gives the sinner the right to believe that all its glorious promises are for him.

DIVINE FOREORDINATION DOES NOT RULE OUT HUMAN ACCOUNTABILITY

Fourthly, divine foreordination does not rule out human action and human accountability: if it did, we would all live in a state of utter paralysis, unable to take a single step until we were sure it was foreordained. After all, foreordination is not confined to spiritual matters such as the conversion of a sinner. It embraces 'whatsoever comes to pass', and the only way we can ever be sure that an act has been foreordained is by doing it. Spurgeon made the point in a characteristic illustration, recalling what 'a brother in Cornwall' said to

---

2   James Durham, *Christ Crucified* (Edinburgh: 1683), p. 7.

3   Ibid.

Malachi, 'a rather stout Calvinist.' 'Now, Malachi, I owe you £2, but before I give it to you I need to know whether I am predestinated to pay you.' Malachi opened wide his hand, and said, 'Put the £2 there, and I will tell you directly.'[4] The same principle applies to every event in our daily lives.

A few Sundays ago as I sat in church listening to the announcements before the service, I learned that there was to be a congregational outing. It promised to be a great day, and the minister stressed that all were welcome. But then it occurred to me: How many of those who have heard this invitation are going to say, 'I would love to go, but I don't know if I'm one of those predestined to go.' None, I concluded. It's only when confronted by the gospel that people seem to raise this sort of argument. We never seem to ask whether it has been foreordained that we should get up in the morning or whether it has been foreordained that we should go to work or to the Cup Final. We simply get up and go.

Or, to put it more seriously, would we think of disregarding the commandment to love our neighbour until we are sure that we have been predestinated to such obedience? No! and it makes no more sense for a hearer of the gospel to put off believing in Christ till she has assured herself that she is one of God's elect, predestined to eternal life. She cannot

---

4   C. H. Spurgeon, *The Treasury of the New Testament* (4 vols., London: Marshall, Morgan and Scott, no date), Vol. 2, p. 357.

suspend her response to the message until she has ascertained that her name has been written in the Book of Life from all eternity; nor can she suspend it till she has checked whether on the Last Day she is to be a sheep or a goat. She has to go by the information available to her, which is, that in the here-and-now God calls her to repentance and commands her to believe; that Christ is offering Himself to her to be her Saviour; that if she comes to Him He will not on any account close the door against her; that when she comes, there will be joy in the presence of the angels; and that it is not only her right, but her duty (like every other sinner) to believe the gospel the moment she hears it. She is not being told to go home and think about it, or that she must deal with this issue before she dies. Christ is Lord and Saviour now. She is a sinner now. She must come now. There must be no trifling and no procrastination, because if we die in unbelief and impenitence we shall most certainly be lost.

But just as the hearer is responsible for responding to the gospel, so is the preacher responsible for making it known. God's foreordination, God's secret counsel, cannot be the rule of his duty, or an excuse for not carrying out his commission. When called by the church to a particular sphere of service he cannot defer his decision until he is sure that God has predestined him to go there; nor until he has been assured that God has foreordained a great harvest for him in that particular sphere. Isaiah clearly had a foreordained ministry, yet he has to lament that no-one has believed his message (Isa. 53:1); and while the ministry of William Chalmers Burns as a missionary to China was undoubtedly divinely foreordained, his incessant and self-denying toil yielded but a meagre harvest of converts in stark contrast to the power which accompanied his preaching in Dundee, Kilsyth and elsewhere in Scotland during the years 1839-41.

But least of all can the preacher limit himself to offering Christ and the promises of the gospel only to the elect. He has no means of knowing that any unconverted person is one of God's chosen. All he does know is that everyone of his hearers is a sinner, that Christ came to save sinners, and that he as a preacher has been sent to place Christ before them, earnestly and importunately. His field is not the elect, but the world (Matt. 13:38); and it is by preaching the whole Christ to the whole world that God gathers His elect. He has told us plainly that He has foreordained a great harvest, but He has not told us whether this particular seeker, or this man filled with remorse, or this plain, ordinary sinner, or this poor drug-addict, is to be part of it. Nor has He told us whether our ministry will be as mightily blessed as Peter's on the Day of Pentecost or yield such a tiny harvest as Paul's in Athens. From a human point of view, we draw at a venture, or not at all.

Every Christian preacher knows that his labour will be in vain apart from the sovereign grace of God, who alone can give force to our words, open the human heart and persuade it to let the Saviour in. This is why prayer is such an important part of the work of an evangelist: so much so that we might even say that a special gift of prayer is part of his distinctive calling. Sometimes, however, this is taken to an extreme, as if it meant that the evangelist himself were nothing at all and that any recognition of the value of his labours would serve only to puff him up. But God doesn't convert people by magic, nor does He force or coerce them into faith. His grace works by persuasion, using the truth as His instrument and the preacher as His agent.

Any right-minded preacher will immediately give God all the glory for any power attending his ministry, but he will also recognise the honour God has put upon him by calling him into His service and blessing his work. This is why Paul's list of the gifts with which Christ has blessed His church places 'evangelists' immediately after apostles and prophets, and before pastor-teachers (Eph. 4:11). But it is also why the same apostle describes those converted through his ministry as his 'joy and crown' (Phil. 4:1) and takes a legitimate pride in the subsequent lives of those he has led to the Lord. In 2 Corinthians 9:2 he even confesses to boasting to the Macedonians about his Corinthian converts; in 2 Corinthians 6:13 he refers to them as his 'children'; and in 2 Corinthians 7:4 he declares that he has great pride in them. These converts, the result of his ministry, are his 'letters of recommendation' (2 Cor. 3:1, 2): what an older generation of Scottish preachers would have called 'seals on their ministry' or 'souls for their hire'.

But the Apostle is also generous in recognising the value of the work done by his fellow-labourers. In 2 Corinthians 8:18 he commends a brother (unknown to us, but obviously well-known to the Corinthians) who is praised by all the churches for his service to the gospel; in verse 23 of the same chapter he speaks of other unnamed brothers who were an honour to Christ; in Philippians 4:3 he commends 'Clement and the rest of my fellow-workers, whose names are in the book of life'; and in the closing greetings of the Epistle to the Romans he speaks warmly of Phoebe, who has been a great help to many people; of Aquila and Priscilla, to whom all the churches of the Gentiles were grateful; of Andronicus and Junias, who were 'outstanding among the apostles'; of Apelles, 'tested and approved in Christ'; and of Tryphena and Tryphosa, 'women who work hard in the Lord.'

The assumption underlying all these compliments (for that is what they are) is that, while all Christian workers operate within the foreordination of God, they are also free and responsible agents, and as such liable to both praise and blame. Where blame was appropriate, Paul would administer it, as he did when he opposed Peter to his face for his dissimulation at Antioch (Gal. 2:11). But when praise was appropriate, the Apostle would dispense it by the spade-full;

knowing he could safely leave it to the world (and to envious fellow-believers) to keep his fellow-workers humble even when God richly blessed them.

Persuaders, not merely proclaimers

Clearly, then, it is through human workers that God normally fulfils His saving purpose; and, equally clearly, He has commissioned these workers to be not only proclaimers, but persuaders. The various New Testament descriptions of the business of an evangelist all make this plain. The first disciples, for example, were called to be 'fishers of men', a phrase which prompted Thomas Boston's *Soliloquy on the Art of Man-Fishing*, composed as he prepared for his ordination to the ministry in 1699.[5] The key point of the comparison between preacher and fisherman, as Boston draws it, is that just as it is the life-work of the fisherman to catch fish so it is the life-work of the preacher to catch souls. To this work he gives his whole strength, and even when he is not actively engaged in it he is still reflecting on it, thinking of what he's been doing and wondering how he could do it better.

Boston's description of man-fishing as an 'art' is fascinating. It is a thing of beauty, requiring imagination as well as labour and toil; and, like any aspiring artist, the evangelist must study the masters, especially the Master

---

5   See *The Complete Works of the Late Rev. Thomas Boston* (12 Vols, 1853. Reprinted Stoke-on-Trent: Tentmaker Publications, 2002), Vol. 5, pp. 5–43.

Himself, the Lord Jesus Christ, and His way of catching souls. The fisherman must know the species he is targeting, the waters they swim in, and the places where they hide. And the work requires its own special net, the net of God's Word of peace and reconciliation, specially designed to catch all sorts of sinners, 'for God excludes none from the benefits of the gospel that will not exclude themselves; it is free to all.'[6] With this net, the fisher of souls sets out in all kinds of weather; he casts it wherever he knows there are sinners; he despairs of the conversion of none, because of his firm belief that the Holy Spirit can drive even the most profligate sinner into his net; and he perseveres whatever the discouragements. Sometimes a fish will touch the net and swim away; other times one will seem to be caught, but struggles and gets loose; at yet other times, a fish he thinks he has landed slips away never to be seen again; and sometimes there are periods, perhaps long periods, when he toils and catches nothing.

The true evangelist can never simply shrug off such discouragements. He will recognise, of course, the sovereignty of God in the conversion of sinners, but even so he finds it hard to acquiesce in periods when his labour is fruitless. He will complain, 'Lord, no-one has believed my message' (Isa. 53:1), and he will protest, 'Lord, how long?' (Isa. 6:11);

---

6   *Ibid*, p. 11.

but he will also ask, 'What have I got wrong?' Perhaps, he muses, it's the meshes of the net. Are they too wide, the warnings and invitations too vague and general, leaving the conscience untouched and allowing the fish to swim blithely through? Or, maybe, too narrow, the preaching so subtle and intricate that the fish quickly turn away? The evangelist always has room for repentance.

St Paul was certainly an outstanding practitioner of the art of man-fishing, but in his Second Epistle to the Corinthians he uses another, very different, metaphor to describe his work. 'I feel a divine jealousy for you,' he writes, 'since I betrothed you to one husband, to present you as a pure virgin to Christ' (2 Cor. 11:2, ESV). Here, the preacher's commission is to bring Christ and the soul together in marriage. This theme was taken up by Robert Leighton in his commentary on the words of 1 Peter 1:8 (NKJV), 'whom having not seen you love.' 'Ministers,' writes Leighton, 'ought to be suitors, not for themselves but for Christ, to espouse souls to him, and to bring in many hearts to love him.'[7] They are wooers, seeking to persuade people to fall in love with Christ, and the remarkable thing here is that they are trying to make them fall in love with someone they have never seen. Like faith, this love comes by hearing, as the preacher commends

---

7   Robert Leighton, *A Practical Commentary upon the First Epistle General of Saint Peter* (2 Vols, 1693–94. Reprinted London: The Religious Tract Society, no date), Vol. 1, p. 106.

to his audience the beauty and majesty of Christ, and His suitability as a spiritual bridegroom, not only for the church (as in Ephesians 5:32), but for the individual. There is so much to tell: His eternal glory as one who was in the form of God; His condescension, making Himself poor so that we, by His poverty, might be made rich; His compassion towards all who were in distress; His love, driving Him to endure the cross in order to atone for our sin; His resurrection, ensuring that He lives for ever to progress and complete His work of salvation; His assurance that if we come to Him there is no way that He will turn us away; His unsearchable riches, all ours in Him; His promise to lead us home to His Father's house; and so much more. He is the Supreme Good, and human restlessness finds rest in Him.

But the suitor cannot be content with merely stating the case for his Master. When Abraham's servant was sent to find a wife for Isaac (Gen. 24:1-66) and was led to Rebekah, he certainly spoke eloquently in commendation of the prospective bridegroom. He came, he said, from a wealthy family and was heir to its fortune; and in token of this the servant brought out gold, jewellery, and articles of clothing for Rebekah; and costly gifts for her family. But his mission was urgent, and brooked no delay, and so Rebekah was quickly asked for a decision: 'Will you go with this man?' 'I will go,' she replied. In the same way the Christian preacher cannot be content with mere exposition of the beauty of

Christ, no matter how profound or moving. His business is to arrange a marriage between the soul and Christ, and so, with all the earnestness he can command, he too must press the question, 'Will you go with this man?' He wants the sinner and Christ to become one flesh, and he wants it for everyone within the sound of his voice.

The third metaphor we have for the Christian preacher is that of an ambassador (2 Cor. 5:18-20). He is a minister of reconciliation: a reminder that the greatest problem we face as human beings is the problem of our relationship with God. There has been a complete breakdown. Our sins have come between us and our Maker and brought us under a fearful condemnation; and left to ourselves we neither could nor would have done anything to mend the relationship. But God, the offended one, has taken the initiative, and acted in Christ to reconcile the world to Himself; or, as it is put in Colossians 1:20, He has made peace by the blood of the cross. Behind these words lies the greatest mystery imaginable: the self-sacrifice of God on behalf of sinners; God humbling Himself by becoming man; God suffering as man and for man on the cross of Calvary; God becoming our sin, and we becoming His righteousness (2 Cor. 5:21).

Now the Apostle stands forth as a servant of that reconciliation, authorised as God's accredited representative to announce to the world that God is for peace; and not only so, but that he is *suing* for peace. The language Paul uses here is utterly remarkable. He has clearly not been warned to be careful as to his choice of language and to avoid any form of words that might seem to compromise the high majesty of an imperious heaven. Quite the contrary! His instructions are to 'appeal' to sinners, and to 'implore' them to avail themselves of peace with God on His terms. And what are these terms? Grace, rich and free, leaving us with nothing to do but to take God at His word, to believe that in Christ He Himself made atonement for our sins on the cross of Calvary, and to accept His offer of free forgiveness, perfect righteousness and everlasting peace. Christ became our sin. We become His righteousness.

Here, through His ambassadors, the Creator is entreating the creature; the All-Holy pleading with the sinner, using the sort of language we usually associate with importunate prayer. It is the language of earnestness, of love, of longing, and it is not only a mandate for passionate evangelism, but a demand for it. There can be no dispassionate proclamation of the gospel. St Paul's heart was in his mission, and so must ours be, because God's heart is in it too.

3

The Free Offer and Limited Atonement

But what of the doctrine of limited atonement: the belief that Christ died not for all, but only for the elect? How, we are asked, can we offer Christ and His salvation to all, when we know that He didn't die for all; or, conversely, how can we offer Christ to all without giving the impression that He died for all; and, most seriously of all, how can we believe in the doctrine of limited atonement and still retain our evangelistic zeal?

Our immediate response to this must be, once again, that as a matter of simple historical fact, some of the most zealous and effective preachers in the history of the church have been firm believers in the doctrine of limited atonement, yet this never prevented them from believing that Christ was to be preached to the whole world; nor from promising categorically that whoever believed in Him would be saved; nor from shedding tears as they pled with sinners to put their trust in the blood of the Lamb. The names of Whitefield, Edwards and Spurgeon immediately come to mind, but others quickly follow. Some, like David Dickson of Irvine, Robert Murray McCheyne of Dundee, and John MacDonald of Ferintosh, were instruments of memorable revivals in their native Scotland; others, like Gilbert Tennent, preached with equal power in New England. Some, such as David Brainerd, Alexander Duff and William Chalmers Burns became heroic pioneer missionaries. In twentieth-century London, the greatest evangelistic pulpit was that of Dr Martyn Lloyd-Jones; and in thousands of churches across the world Calvinist preachers whose names have long since been forgotten laboured as earnest soul-winners.

How can we explain this? First of all, by the fact that such men heard in the Christian Scriptures not only a voice that proclaimed that Christ had loved His church and given Himself for her, but also, and no less clearly, a voice that commanded them to bring the good news about Christ to the notice of every creature. It was none of their business to reconcile the two voices. Their duty was to believe the one, and to obey the other.

Secondly, far from being paralysed by the doctrine of limited atonement they knew that their labour could not be in vain because out in that great wide world there was a multitude that Christ had bought with His blood. They were Christ's sheep (John 10:16) and it was the preacher's job, working under the Chief Shepherd, to gather them. The blood of the Son of God could not have been shed in vain. It had been shed to bring to God an innumerable multitude of His choosing, and it could not fail of its purpose.

Thirdly, these preachers knew that it was by the free offer of the gospel that they themselves had been led to Christ and salvation, and they were sure that the same was true of almost all their Christian friends. They knew that their faith was a gift from God, but they also knew that it was the fruit of clear and earnest preaching: preaching which had set forth the beauty of Christ and had assured them that He was there for them, as poor sinners, to come to, no matter how unworthy they might feel. They owed it to their neighbours to share that same gospel with them, and in the same terms.

Fourthly, they knew that the blood of Christ, the Son of God, was fully sufficient to atone for the sins of the whole world (and, they would have added, of many worlds besides); and not only did they know this, but they believed that the whole world had a right to know it. Christ had taken flesh and blood, and every flesh-and-blood sinner had a right to Him which no angel could ever have. He was Mediator for the human race, the one and only Mediator, and every human had a right to avail themselves of His services as Prophet, Priest and King. Similarly, He was the expiation and propitiation for the sins of the whole world (1 John 2:2), and every man and woman had the right to come to His cross confessing their sins and seeking forgiveness through His blood. They might not avail themselves of it, but the right was theirs, and the faithful preacher would plead with all his hearers to claim it. He would tell them that no stain of sin was so deep that the Blood could not cleanse it, no sinner so contemptible that the Advocate would turn them away, and no shame so overwhelming that it should reduce us to spiritual paralysis and despair. Hope was to be given to every sinner. The love of God was wide enough, the price paid handsome enough, the Spirit's power great enough. They would extend the universal invitation, 'Come!', and they would repeat, once again, the assurance, 'None are excluded but those who exclude themselves.'

Fifthly, these Reformed preachers went forth boldly to offer Christ to the whole world because they had a glorious gospel to preach, whether to religion's cultured despisers or to Edinburgh's 'ragged boys' or to head-hunters beyond the seas. At first sight, of course, it didn't look as glorious as the Arminian gospel. After all, the Arminian could proclaim that Christ had died for all men, that He had secured redemption for all men, and that the sinner had 'only' to believe, and the redemption would be his.

But how could the sinner, dead in his sins, ever come to believe? And supposing that, simply by exercising his own free will, he did achieve the grace of faith, is it not true (according to Arminianism) that he could fall from that grace at any time, and thus never inherit eternal life? His 'decision for Christ' might ultimately be in vain. By any standards this is truly a limited redemption, making no provision to ensure that anyone actually comes to enjoy the forgiveness purchased by Christ or that, even if they do, they will persevere in it to the end.

The Calvinist or Reformed understanding of redemption is completely different. It means a complete and total salvation: not one limited to mere forgiveness; not one that leaves it up to the enslaved human will whether anyone will ever come to Christ; and not one which left it an open question whether, having come to faith, we will persevere to the end. On the contrary, it was a redemption which secured for sinners 'everything we need for life and godliness' (2 Pet. 1:3). It made absolutely certain the salvation of a multitude too great to count. They would be effectually called by God Himself to faith and repentance; they would be united to Christ, and in Him reconciled to God; they would be justified and adopted into God's family; they would be sanctified and kept; and they would be raised to a glorious resurrection. None of this was left to the vagaries of the human will. It was what God the Father intended when He gave His Son as a sacrifice for the sins of the world; it was what the Son intended when He gave Himself; and it was what the Holy Spirit intended when He anointed Christ as Saviour and when He upheld Him through the whole course of His ministry. It was what Christ intended during His ministry on earth, and it is what He intends as He continues His ministry in heaven. He lived, and He died, and He rose, to bring His church to God: all the way!

Consider two preachers, the one an Arminian, the other a Calvinist. The former has a real zeal for the conversion of his hearers, assures them that Christ died for them all, and appeals to them all to accept Him as their personal Saviour. He knows (he cannot help knowing) that apart from divine grace no sinner will ever come to saving faith, but he also believes, first, that divine grace will be effective only if the sinner cooperates with it, and, secondly, that this divine grace is not invincible. His hearers can, and will, resist it, even to the point where they eventually say a decisive 'No!' to Christ. Appeal as he will, and draw on the most approved methods of evangelism, he cannot open the door of a single human heart. Indeed, without the sinner's cooperation even God cannot open it. Evangelism thus becomes a battle of wills between the hearer and the preacher, whose only hope is that the sinner himself will open the door and let Christ in. But is that a forlorn hope if the natural man is incapable of understanding the things of the Spirit of God (1 Cor. 2:14) and sees no beauty whatever in Christ (Isa. 53:2)?

What of the Calvinist? He is equally zealous for the conversion of sinners, equally unrestricted in his appeals, and equally forthright in assuring all his hearers that whoever believes will be saved. At the same time he knows that without the Lord his most earnest preaching is in vain. But this is not all he knows. He also knows that by His death on the cross Christ not only purchased redemption for all who would put their faith in Him: He purchased that faith itself for a multitude too numerous to count. Behind the preacher lies the commitment of all three Persons of the Godhead to the salvation of His people. The Son would expiate their sin, the Father would draw them to Christ and the Holy Spirit would open their hearts to welcome the Saviour. The gospel would come to men not only with words, but with power and deep persuasiveness (1 Thess. 1:5).

It was armed with such confidence that the Reformed preacher went forth, sustained by the hope that in every audience to which God sent him there were those whom Christ had died to save and to whom the Holy Spirit would give the gift of faith and repentance.

Or, consider these two preachers from another point of view. Both promise salvation to all who believe. But do they promise the same salvation? The Calvinist promises, 'Believe in the Lord Jesus Christ and you will have eternal life. The moment you put your trust in the mercy of God and in the blood of Christ, all your sins will be forgiven: for ever.' That is a tremendous assurance. But it is not all. He also promises that the moment we put our faith in Christ we can begin to rejoice in hope of the glory of God (Rom. 5:2). The blood has secured our sanctification as well as our justification; our perseverance as well as our conversion; our glorification as well as our regeneration. Faith means placing ourselves in Christ's hands, and no force in earth or hell can ever pluck us out of them (John 10:28-30). It means becoming members of Christ's body, and that body will never lose a single limb. God's love will never let us go. His grace will lead us home.

None of this is to say that God never blesses the preaching of Arminians. The ministry of John Wesley is sufficient proof that He does. Whatever their distaste for the doctrine of invincible grace, he and his many Methodist successors prayed fervently that God would accompany their preaching with power, and the Lord heard them. But what it does mean is that Arminianism still rests everything on the sinner's 'decision for Christ', and still leaves it an open question whether, having made such a decision, he will persevere in following the Lamb. From this point of view the believer who is governed by an Arminian theology can never have full assurance of salvation, because there always hangs over his head the possibility that he will not keep going to the end.

But then, even Calvinists themselves have often failed to grasp the importance of the doctrine of the perseverance of the saints. Too often we have seen it as merely an add-on to the so-called Five Points of Calvinism or just a detail in the controversy with Arminians. In reality, it is one of the great glories of the message of the Reformation: perhaps its greatest glory. At every point, even though 'tossed about with many a conflict, many a doubt,' we can sing with John Newton:

> 'Tis grace hath brought me safe thus far,
> And grace will lead me home.

4

The Free Offer and Divine Sincerity

It goes without saying that every preacher sincerely desires the conversion and salvation of all his hearers; and it should also go without saying that every Christian sincerely desires the salvation of all their neighbours. But can the same be said of God? Does He sincerely desire the salvation of everyone to whom He offers Christ in the gospel? Or does the very fact that He has not decreed the salvation of all men not make plain that He does not desire the salvation of all men, or even the salvation of all to whom Christ is preached?[1]

One of the key texts bearing on this question is Ezekiel 18:23, where we read, 'Do I take any pleasure in the death of the wicked? declares the Sovereign Lord. Rather, am I not pleased when they turn from their ways and live?' The

---

1 On the question whether God can properly be said to desire the salvation of all men, see the article, 'The Free Offer of the Gospel' in *Collected Writings of John Murray* (4 Vols., 1976–82. Edinburgh: Banner of Truth), Vol. 4, pp. 113–32.

question is clearly rhetorical, as if it were absurd to imagine that God could take any pleasure in the death of the wicked, and the phrase 'the wicked' is all-embracing. He does not take pleasure in the death of a single wicked person. What does give Him pleasure is when the wicked turn from their way, choose life, and cast themselves on His mercy; and when they do so, all heaven celebrates (Luke 15:10). A penitent sinner gives a joy which no angel can ever give to its Maker, and then all the angels rejoice with Him. But why does the death and condemnation of the wicked give God no pleasure?

First, because of His love for the whole human race, including His enemies. We have the highest possible authority for such a doctrine: the words of the Lord Himself in Matthew 5:43-47. Here Jesus is laying down as one of the great guiding principles of discipleship the obligation to love our enemies; and to reinforce the lesson He appeals to the example of God Himself, who sends His sun to shine on the evil as well as on the good and causes His rain to fall on the unrighteous as well as on the righteous. True, sun and rain are not spiritual blessings: they are blessings of Common Grace, but the point the Lord is making is that they flow from a universal divine love. The sun shines on the wicked because God loves them, even though they are His enemies, and the most God-like thing that we can do is to show our enemies the same love (*agape*) that God shows toward ourselves. His attitude toward the whole human race is one of care and benevolence. This is why He wishes the good news of Christ to be preached to every creature. This is why He has provided an atonement sufficient for the sins of the whole world (1 John 2:2). This is why He pleads with us to be reconciled to Him (2 Cor. 5:20) and this is why He promises that He will welcome every returning prodigal with open arms.

In line with this, the Bible portrays God as shrinking from executing judgment even where it is fully deserved. This point is made most memorably through the prophet Hosea when God confronts the idolatrous unfaithfulness of His people Israel (Hos. 11:8-9). He knows what they deserve: the full fury of His anger. But He is torn between His sense of justice and His love for Israel. Their sin is as great as that of Admah and Zeboim, the Cities of the Plain, but God's compassion is stirred and He cries, 'How can I give you up, Ephraim? How can I hand you over, Israel?' His heart recoils from treating them as they deserve, and He concludes, 'I will not carry out my fierce anger, nor devastate Ephraim again.' Why? Is it because His actions at this point are less than God-like? Quite the contrary, as He himself makes plain: 'For I am God, and not man – the Holy One among you. I will not come in wrath.' God, as God, forgives with joy and enthusiasm. He condemns only with reluctance; only in the face of impenitence.

When we turn to the New Testament we find it using language reminiscent of Ezekiel and Hosea. Take 2 Peter 3:9, where the Apostle grounds God's patience towards the human race in the fact that He does not want anyone to perish but desires that everyone should come to repentance. 'This,' writes Calvin, 'is his wondrous love towards the human race, that he desires all men to be saved, and is prepared to bring even the perishing to safety.'[2] St Paul expresses the same sentiment, but this time positively, in 1 Timothy 2:4, where he writes, '[God our Saviour] wants all men to be saved and to come to a knowledge of the truth.' Some Calvinists, in their anxiety to protect the doctrine of election, have urged that the phrase 'all men' must be taken to refer not to all human beings indiscriminately, but to 'all sorts and conditions of men'. This, they claim, suits the context, where Paul was addressing a specific problem, namely, a tendency among his persecuted readers to regard the ruling classes as beyond redemption, and therefore not to be prayed for. Over against this the Apostle lays down, they say, that God's saving will embraces all ranks of the human race, including kings and all in authority, as well as the lower classes who then made up the vast majority of Christian disciples.

---

2   John Calvin, *The Epistle of Paul the Apostle to the Hebrews and the First and Second Epistles of St Peter*, tr. William B. Johnston (Grand Rapids: Eerdmans, 1994), p. 364.

However, although the specific command here is that Christians are not to hold back from praying for those in positions of power, the command is rooted in the more fundamental truth that God desires 'all men' to be saved. The phrase (Greek, *tous anthrōpous*) is unambiguous, and Paul has already used it in the opening verse of the chapter to enjoin us to pray for all human beings, simply as such; and just as we are called on to pray for the salvation of all men so, writes Calvin, 'God has at heart the salvation of all men.'[3] This is why He commands us to pray for all human beings, why He commands His church to preach the gospel to all, why He commands all who hear it to believe it, and why He promises that all who believe it will be saved. Every one of these details speaks of divine grace, but they speak equally clearly of our human responsibility. It is the responsibility of the church to share God's desire that all men be saved, and in pursuance of this to evangelise the whole world. It is the responsibility of every nation and community to keep its doors open to the gospel. And it is the responsibility of all who hear the gospel to receive it with joy.

It is precisely because God so earnestly desires our salvation that our rejection of it grieves Him so deeply; and we can see just how deeply from the anguished cry of the Saviour Himself, 'O Jerusalem, Jerusalem, you who kill

---

3   *Ibid*, p. 208.

the prophets and stone those sent to you, how often I have longed to gather your children together, as a hen gathers her chicks under her wings, but you were not willing' (Matt. 23:37). Down through the ages, Jerusalem had been 'the slayer of prophets' (v. 37), and as Jesus speaks, He knows that He Himself, the last in the line, is shortly to suffer the same fate. Having slain the servants, they are now about to slay the Son (Matt. 21:33-38). But if the denunciations recorded in the earlier part of the chapter (Matt. 23:13-36) reflect the Lord's anger against His own people's treatment of God's messengers, they also reflect His distress as He contemplates the judgment that is to fall on them: their city and their land will become a desolation, and the depth of the Lord's feeling is reflected in the repeated, 'O Jerusalem, Jerusalem,' reminiscent of David's grief when he cried, 'O my son Absalom! My son, my son Absalom! If only I had died instead of you, Absalom, my son, my son' (2 Sam. 18:33). And die for them was exactly what Jesus was about to do (John 11:50).

But how often, Jesus recalls, 'have I longed to gather your children together, as a hen gathers her chicks under her wings.' In what capacity is He speaking here? Some have insisted that He is speaking purely as a man, expressing no more than a natural human compassion for people about to be overwhelmed by calamity and tragedy, in which case

His lament tells us nothing about the inner feelings of transcendent deity.

There is certainly humanity here. These were His own people, this was His city, and He was moved to the depths of His human being by the vision He had of the cruelty and destruction to be inflicted on it by the Roman soldiery in 70AD. But there is more here than the voice of humanity. No mere man could have offered to gather a whole nation together under His wings. He speaks as the Messiah, as the Son of God, and although His glory is obscured by the veil of His humanity He is still the revelation of God, even to the extent that He can say that whoever has seen Him (or heard Him) has seen and heard the Father (John 14:9). In this lament, as in all else, He and the Father are one, otherwise Christ's status as God's last Word (Heb. 1:2) is dangerously undermined.

The image of the Lord as a mother-hen is indeed a homely one, but this is typical of God's condescension, as is the portrayal of God as a shepherd seeking a lost sheep or a housewife turning her home upside down in the search for a lost coin (Luke 15:3-10). Besides, there is a close parallel to the mother-hen image in Psalm 91:4, where we read, 'He will cover you with his feathers, and under his wings you will find refuge.' There can be no doubt that the 'wings' referred to here are God's wings: verse 4 is simply amplifying the point made in verse 1, which describes the believer as dwelling in the shadow of the Almighty. There is another parallel in Deuteronomy 32:11, where Moses compares the Lord to an eagle hovering protectively over its young. Again, there can be no doubt that the 'eagle' here is God, and Jesus' image of the mother-hen bespeaks the same divine solicitude. Few of His hearers would ever have seen an eagle, but all were familiar with the sight of the mother-hen alarmed by the sparrow-hawk hovering menacingly, quickly summoning her brood, and they scurrying at once to find shelter, huddled closely together, under her wings. No predator was going to mess with her.

That is what Jesus, Messiah, Mediator and Saviour, had longed to do. He knew the danger, not only temporal but spiritual, that men were in, and He had called them to Himself, there to find safety, security and comfort. This had driven His earthly ministry from the very beginning, as He traversed the land from end to end, and from village to city, preaching, healing, praying and weeping. He had set before them the mercy of God, He had pointed them to the strait gate and the narrow way, He had set before them the prospect of eternal life, and He had warned them of the wrath to come.

But this was not all. The Lord's work as Saviour had not begun with His birth at Bethlehem. It was He who, as the pre-incarnate Mediator, had sent prophet after prophet and who had pled with His people, 'Turn! Turn from your evil

ways! Why will you die, O house of Israel?' (Ezek. 33:11).
He had sent a Moses to instruct them, an Isaiah to proclaim
good news, a Jeremiah to weep; and now, here He was in
person, God in the flesh, visible, audible, wooing, warning,
pleading. But it was all to no avail. He had come to His
own people, dwelling among them in grace and truth, but
they had rejected Him. The chicks had refused to heed the
warnings of the mother-hen.

There can be no doubting the sincerity of the Lord's
feelings at this point. Nor can we doubt that they reflect the
heart of His deity no less than the heart of His humanity.
His longing for the salvation of His hearers was that of one
who, conscious of His own powers, had earlier offered rest
to all the world's weary (Matt. 11:28); and His anguish
was exactly that of the One who had cried through His
prophet, Hosea, 'How can I give you up, Ephraim? … All
my compassion is aroused' (Hos. 11: 8).

But then, neither can there be any doubt as to where the
blame lies. 'I was willing,' says the Lord, 'but you were not
willing.' We must allow these words their full force. From
the very beginning, God has given human beings the space
to make their own decisions, and we have used that space
to defy Him. But such freedom brings accountability, and
the evangelist must constantly challenge his hearers with
what they already know to be the truth, namely, that they
themselves bear the whole responsibility for refusing God's

offer of life through Christ. The preacher must pin that word to their consciences: *Unwilling!* 'You get no wrong,' wrote James Durham, 'when you get your own choice.'[4]

---

4   James Durham, *Christ Crucified*, p. 13.

5

Delivering the Free Offer

If our commission is, as we have seen, to bring our hearers to put their faith in Christ, then our priority must be to persuade them that He fully deserves their faith, and the only way to do this is to make His person and His work the great recurring theme of our preaching, showing them His glory from every possible angle. This may seem blindingly obvious, but there is always a temptation to assume that if we are calling for faith then what we have to do is describe faith itself. It's doubtful, however, whether the word 'trust' (which is what we're calling for) can be reduced to anything simpler. It's hard to make the advice, 'Trust me,' clearer than it already is, and if we keep on talking about faith there is a real danger that people will come to think that it is in faith itself they are to put their trust.

That rare breed of men whose job it is to repair scarily-high transmitter masts would derive no reassurance from a lecture on trust. What they need to know is whether the ladder is securely fixed, whether the rungs are in good shape and whether the whole arrangement is meticulously maintained. Will it hold? Will it take them safely up, and safely down again? Their faith is in the ladder, not in their faith. The same is true of Christian faith: it puts its trust in Christ, not in itself, and this is why the New Testament majors not on what we have to do but on who Christ was and what Christ did.

More specifically, this is why the Gospels are the great resource of the Christian evangelist. They are all about Christ, and we abuse them if we deploy them instead to provide homilies on, for example, the vagaries of the Christian life. They want to tell us about *Him*: His pre-existence, His miraculous birth, His divine sonship, His compassionate humanity, His mighty acts, His incomparable teaching, His atoning death, His resurrection and ascension, His universal dominion, the promise of His coming again, His eminence as the Supreme Judge on the Last Day.

We find the same pattern in the Epistles. The apostles preach Christ crucified (1 Cor. 1:23) because His cross is the answer to our sins and the supreme demonstration of the love of God; and likewise, in the Book of Revelation, we are never far away from the Lamb in the centre of the throne (Rev. 5:6).

What all this means is that it is by holding up Christ, not by analysing faith, that people are drawn to the Saviour; and this, in turn, means that there can be no call to faith apart from theology; or, more precisely, apart from Christology. Evangelism means proclaiming the Evangel, the good news, and the good news is always Jesus, the one and only Mediator or Go-between between God and humanity: our Prophet, Priest and King; our Physician, Shepherd, Leader, Counsellor, Friend, Brother, Protector, Saviour, Lord, and daily Companion.

It follows from this that evangelism is not something the church does occasionally, or something that well-established churches can leave to special groups charged with the responsibility of planting new churches. It has to be part of the corporate life of every church, though this has to be stated with care. It doesn't mean that conversion must be the aim of every sermon, or that there is neither wisdom nor value in special evangelistic services. Nor does it mean that evangelism should be *confined* to the church's ordinary services: the church must also reach out to those who never come to church (the modern equivalent of those in the 'highways and hedges', Luke 14:23). Nor, yet again, does it mean that every so often we should preach on what might be regarded as special evangelistic texts. The whole Bible is evangelistic. If, for example, we are preaching from, or through, the Gospel of Mark or the Gospel of John or the

Epistle to the Romans we cannot avoid being evangelists, because each of them gives a crystal-clear statement of the gospel.

The same is true of the great doctrines of the Bible. God as Creator, still holding the world in His hands, is a great evangelistic doctrine; sovereign grace is a great evangelistic doctrine; and so are the atonement, and justification by faith, and the new birth, and the perseverance of the saints, and the resurrection life believers already possess in Christ (John 11:25-26). Each one of these is part of the portrait of the one we are urging people to believe in, and any ministry or witnessing Christian community which fails to give proper emphasis to any one of them is diminishing the Evangel (and, by implication, reducing its power). From every one of them there is a direct route to the great evangelistic call and its attendant promise, 'Believe in the Lord Jesus Christ and you will be saved.' It is in the message of the Bible, and in these great doctrines, that men and women are to put their trust.

Yet the question of what we mean when we call for faith in Christ cannot be entirely avoided. In fact, it was one of the key issues in a controversy which agitated the Church in Scotland between 1718 and 1723. The controversy centred on a book called *The Marrow of Modern Divinity*, published in London in 1645. It attracted little notice at the time, but almost sixty years later Thomas Boston came across a copy of the First Part while on a visit to one of his parishioners. At the time he was struggling with what he feared was a note of 'legality' in his own preaching and, as he recalled later, when he discovered the *Marrow* he 'relished it greatly' as 'a light which the Lord had seasonably struck up to me in my darkness.'[1] Soon he was recommending it to his friends, and one of these, the Reverend James Hog of Carnock in Fife, had it republished in 1718 with a recommendatory Preface from his own pen.

The *Marrow* was cast in the form of a conversation between Evangelista, a minister of the gospel, and three others: a legalist, an antinomian, and a young Christian. The conversation is conducted largely by way of extracts from what were then 'modern' theologians: Reformers such as Martin Luther, and English Puritans such as John Preston and William Ames, and although it contained some expressions which might raise the eyebrows of the theologically fastidious, no one had hitherto accused it of heresy, even though it was published in the hey-day of Puritanism, when men like John Owen, Thomas Goodwin and Thomas Manton were at the height of their powers. But in 1720, the General Assembly of the Church of Scotland found in the *Marrow* heresy a-plenty, forbade its ministers

---

1   *Memoirs of the Life, Times and Writings of Thomas Boston of Ettrick. Written by Himself* (1776. New Edition Glsagow: John McNeilage, 1899), p. 160.

to recommend it in any way, and instructed them to warn their people against it.

Among the errors which the Assembly found in the *Marrow* was the doctrine that assurance was of the essence of faith, and one invaluable spin-off from the controversy was that it stirred men like Boston and Ebenezer Erskine to clarify the meaning of saving faith. Their starting-point was the explanation which at one point Evangelista offered to Neophytus, the young Christian: 'Be verily persuaded in your heart that Jesus Christ is yours, and that you shall have life and salvation by him.'[2] The key word here is 'persuaded'. Faith is sure. Faith is convinced. Faith is certain. It is not a state of feeling, but first and foremost a state of the mind.

But of what is faith sure? It is sure that every hearer of the gospel is entitled to say, 'Christ is mine': not in the sense that the preacher can tell every single sinner that he already possesses Christ, but in the sense that in the gospel God is saying, 'He's yours. Take Him; and if you take Him, you will have life and salvation by Him.' This is exactly how it is put in the Shorter Catechism (86): faith receives and rests upon Christ 'as he is offered to us in the gospel'. The offer comes before faith. It makes Christ ours by right, and invites us to make Him ours by possession. Regardless of our feelings, and regardless of our sense of self-worth, it gives us a warrant

---

2   *The Marrow of Modern Divinity*, p. 118.

to take Him as our Saviour. The good news is for *me*! Life and salvation are being held out to me, pressed upon me. Faith has a right to be sure of it, to be really persuaded of it, and to be deeply moved by it because, as St Paul points out, it is a matter of the heart (Rom. 6:17; 10:9). It is not a bare assent to facts and doctrines, with no more impact than our belief that the Battle of Bannockburn was fought in 1314. It is a cordial, joyful, adoring trust (Acts 16:34; 1 Pet. 1:8) because in Christ we find relief and deliverance, release and hope, and an assurance that in Him we are secure for time and eternity.

But faith is also what Boston and his colleagues called an 'appropriating persuasion'. The mere offer will not save us. Our right to Him will not save us. We must take Him, and that is what faith does. It is sure of Him; and it takes Him. It grasps the gift. It takes a grip of it, and in that grip Christ is wholly and fully mine, not only in the sense that I have a right to life and salvation in Him, but in the sense that I now *possess* life and salvation; and having once taken possession, I can never lose it. He is mine for ever. My sins are for ever forgiven; the life of God in my soul will never die.

These are the great truths that Boston and his friends suffered for; and never were they more needed than at the present time.

SHOULD WE FORGET OUR CALVINISM AND PREACH LIKE ARMINIANS?

But what of the idea that when preaching evangelistically we should forget our Calvinism and preach like Arminians? The short answer is that it is an idea born of a caricature. The Calvinist, so the perception goes, has no passion, no earnestness; or, more dismissively still, the Calvinist never preaches a gospel which is free and for all. But John Knox had certainly not left his Calvinism behind when he was taking his passion out on his poor pulpit, and 'dinging it into blads'; nor had Thomas Boston when he preached his sermon, 'Present Room for Sinners in Christ's House,'[3] anticipating by more than a hundred years the African-American spiritual, 'Gospel Train Coming,' with its great refrain, 'There's room for many a-more'; and neither had George Whitefield when his preaching drew 20,000 people to Cambuslang in July 1742; or C. H. Spurgeon when he preached his great 'Compel them to Come In' sermon.

Far from abandoning his Calvinism in order to facilitate his evangelism, the Reformed preacher ventured forth sustained by the hope that in every audience he addressed there were some whom God had ordained to eternal life; and by the hope that his 'poor, lisping, stammering tongue' might become the means of an effectual divine call through

3   Thomas Boston, *Works,* Vol. 3, 260–72.

which the Father would draw to the Son those whom He had loved from all eternity and whom He had been tracking since the day they were born. And, precisely because he was a Calvinist, he knew that invincible grace can open any heart, give peace to the most troubled conscience, and make the foulest clean. Today we should still know that Christ stands at our elbow, and that precisely this audience, numbering perhaps no more than a dozen, and gathered in a small, cold hall, has been part of God's plan from the beginning, as have the text we expect to preach from, and the sermon we hope to deliver. God will weave them into His own bright design.

But there is one danger peculiar to the Calvinist preacher: he may be overly concerned to guard himself against the risk of coming under suspicion as a man tainted with Arminianism. It reminds me of an experience shared with me by an older minister of the last generation. He was a man noted both for the passion with which he preached and for the divine blessing that rested on his ministry, but one evening as he was pouring his whole soul (and his body too) into an earnest appeal to the unconverted, he suddenly realised that such preaching had its critics and that he was probably providing grist for their mill. Unabashed, and in no mood to compromise, he boldly declared, 'And if that's Arminianism, I'm full of it!' But it wasn't, and he knew it wasn't, otherwise he would never have indulged in it. But it would be foolish to imagine that the fear of man never constrains our freedom. Many a man who inwardly believes firmly in the free offer will choose his words carefully, too carefully, to make sure he keeps a safe distance between himself and the theological precipice. Such caution can take many forms.

I have seen preachers who believed with all their hearts that Christ was to be offered freely to all, but hold back on it because they knew that in the congregation there was someone who prided himself on his 'discernment' and frowned on preachers who were 'too free' with the gospel. It might be a fellow minister, or a censorious elder, or the sort of Christian (perhaps even a recent convert) who goes to church not to hear the gospel, but to hear if you have it. We have to be absolutely clear in our response to this. The free offer of the gospel is not some minor doctrine which may be sacrificed for the sake of peace or suppressed in order to protect some other more important doctrine. No doctrine is more important than the free offer. To deny it is not simply to engage in some minor theological disagreement. It is heresy. Martin Luther once said that if the doctrine of justification is lost, the whole of the gospel is lost. But if it is the case that it is the ungodly that God justifies (as Luther believed) then it is precisely to the ungodly, all the ungodly without exception, that God's way of forgiveness and reconciliation is to be preached. Every properly educated preacher should know that far from being a threat to Calvinism, the free offer lies at its very heart, as the Synod of Dort made plain. And every Calvinist has to ask himself this question: who is more important, that well-known sermon-taster, straining to catch the faintest whiff of Arminianism, or the poor sinner whose eternal well-being depends on his being introduced to Christ?

But the feeling that we must protect ourselves against the suspicion of heresy can also take another form. Imagine a preacher who for thirty or forty-five minutes has been delivering a sermon full of the gospel and full of Christ, and with constant application to the unconverted, urging them to come to Christ 'just as I am'. But then, at the very end, he remembers, 'Predestination! I must safeguard predestination;' and so, in a few clumsy sentences, he nullifies the impact of all he has been saying about the outstretched arms of Jesus and the urgency of instant compliance with the gospel-call, and gives his hearers a perfect excuse to go home and do nothing.

This is why Thomas Chalmers once remarked that it was less important to protect such doctrines as predestination and limited atonement than to guard against the abuse of them, and we are certainly abusing them if they come between us and proclaiming in Christ's name, 'Come to me, and I will give you rest.' Surely the point is that every text must be allowed to proclaim its own distinctive message? If we are preaching on Romans 8:28-30 we must bring out all it has to say on sovereign grace and predestination, making plain that our salvation stems from the free initiative of God's love (bearing in mind that the point Paul is making is not that *only* the elect will be saved, but that *all* the elect will be saved). Conversely, if we are preaching from John 3:16, our duty is to highlight the wonder of God's love and to make plain to everyone who belongs to the 'world' that Christ is there for them to come to. This is why it is important that preachers should have a solid theological education. Without it, uncertainty as to what is heresy and what is orthodoxy can all too easily paralyse their ministry. The preacher must be sure of his ground.

THE COST OF DISCIPLESHIP

But if the evangelist is under orders to highlight the beauty of Christ and His salvation, he is also under orders not to hide the cost of discipleship. There is a real danger here, especially if we become obsessed with statistics and come to see ourselves as recruiting sergeants. Someone once remarked that you never see legless soldiers paraded at an army recruiting station, and it's equally tempting for us to preach Christ as the way to happiness-ever-after, keeping well out of sight the cost of the spiritual warfare that is to follow. This was certainly not the Lord's way. Instead, He laid down that, 'Whoever wants to be my disciple must deny themselves and take up their cross' (Matt. 16:24), and

He went on to spell it out in detail. They would receive from the world the same treatment as it had meted out to their Master. Following Him could cost people their lives (Matt. 16:25), it would expose them to hatred and persecution (Matt. 10:16-23), it might lead them to being forced to choose between Christ and their parents or between Christ and their children (Matt. 10:37).

St Paul was equally unequivocal. Far from preaching a version of the modern Prosperity Gospel he made plain that Christians will not be exempt from the sufferings of the present age (Rom. 8:18). He warned Timothy of 'terrible times' to come (2 Tim. 3:1), declared that 'everyone who wants to live a godly life in Christ' will be persecuted (2 Tim. 3:12) and left him in no doubt that in the course of his work as an evangelist he would have to endure hardship (2 Tim. 4.5).

The Book of Revelation bears the same message. Those from whose eyes God eventually wipes away every tear have all had to come through the great tribulation (Rev. 7:14). This is why the Book of Psalms has been so precious to Christian believers down the ages. It is strikingly honest in portraying the life of the righteous man as beset by many troubles (Ps. 34:19); and when we find ourselves in the depths (Ps. 130:1) and in fearful pits (Ps. 40:2) the psalms give us the very words in which to pour forth our laments and our prayers.

Sometimes the pressure to win converts can lead to what James Packer calls 'a scalp-hunting zeal in evangelism'[4] and this, in turn, can betray us into painting a deceptively rosy picture of the Christian life. Evangelism then degenerates all too easily into a kind of election campaign in which people are urged to 'decide for Christ' or to 'choose Christ' as the candidate who offers the best deal; which, of course, Christ does, but unlike political candidates He doesn't deceive us. Instead, He is scrupulously honest. The Christian life is not a convalescent home, but a battlefield on which we face daily the combined ferocity, cunning and malice of the world, the flesh and the devil. The Broad Way has to be forsaken, the old man crucified, some relationships abandoned, and many a personal ambition set aside. We have to come to terms with the shame attached to the gospel (Rom. 1:16) and with the fact that we face painful discipline when we defy God's house-rules.

This highlights the great advantage of an evangelism rooted in the regular life and worship of a congregation where an expository ministry covers the 'whole counsel of God', including the reality of suffering as a part of Christian discipleship. That means that there are no false expectations. By contrast, any conversion secured by the promise of life-long *Hallelujahs!* will end only in disillusionment and

---

4   J. I. Packer, *Evangelism and the Sovereignty of God*, p. 80.

apostasy; or in the anguished protest, 'You never told me it would be like this!' But the Bible very plainly did; and our evangelism must do the same.

But if it is important to make plain the cost of discipleship it is no less important to stress that conversion is but the entry-point to a course of lifelong learning. Modern Evangelicalism, going back to men like George Whitefield, has rightly emphasised the sinner's need to be born again, but this carries its own dangers, creating the impression that once we're converted, that's it; and along with that, the impression that conversion is the whole aim of the Christian ministry. Here the order of the Great Commission is profoundly instructive: 'Go, make disciples, baptise them, *and* teach them.' This highlights the importance of post-conversion teaching. But it does more than that. It highlights the great need of new converts to be instructed in the principles of Christian living: 'teach them to obey everything I have commanded you.' This is what we see worked out so brilliantly in chapters 4–6 of Paul's Epistle to the Ephesians, where the Apostle develops the theme of 'a life worthy of the calling you have received' (Eph. 4:1); and Jim Packer captures the essence of the Apostle's teaching when he distinguishes between a conversion experience on the one hand and 'convertedness' on the other, adding that the mark of 'convertedness' is that we are 'one of the Lord's *learners*'.[5]

We should leave people in no doubt that this, rather than a one-off conversion experience is the response we are looking for. Our salvation is secure, but not static. Every genuine 'born-again Christian' becomes a little child, and like all little children they need to grow, and to grow they need to be fed. Otherwise they will remain children for ever. They need the milk of the Word. They need the ministry of pastor-teachers. They need the admonition and encouragement of their fellow believers. They need the Lord's Supper. Only by such means and with such support can converts cope with the cost of discipleship and discover the precise form of their own personal call to Christian service; and, above all, only by such means can they have a constantly renewed vision of 'the grace of the Lord Jesus Christ, and the love of God, and the fellowship of the Holy Spirit' (2 Cor. 13:14).

Evangelism a call into the fellowship of the church

It follows from this that evangelism is not only a call to union with Christ but a call into communion with His people, the church. Sadly, this call has been largely eclipsed by the individualism which has overtaken so much of modern

---

5   From the article, 'What is Evangelism?' in *Collected Shorter Writings of J. I. Packer*, (4 Vols., 1998–99; Carlisle: Paternoster), Vol. 2, p. 253.

Christianity. 'One of our chief evangelical blind spots,' wrote John Stott, 'has been to overlook the central importance of the church. We tend to proclaim individual salvation without moving on to the saved community. We think of ourselves more as "Christians" than as "churchmen", and our message is more good news of a new life than of a new society.'[6] As Stott goes on to say, no one can emerge from reading the apostolic documents with such a 'privatised gospel', yet this is exactly what many modern Christians seem to do, even to the extent that it is not uncommon to hear people say, 'I'm a Christian, but I never go to church.'

This would have shocked our spiritual forefathers, and it would have done so because it fundamentally contradicts the pattern we see in Scripture. From the very beginning, Jesus formed His disciples into a community gathered around Himself, and it looks very much as if this reflected His own need for human fellowship. He chose the Twelve, not in the first instance to be His 'apprentices', but 'that they might be with him' (Mark 3:14). They became the nucleus of the church, gradually expanded until, even in his own life-time, it numbered at least five hundred (1 Cor. 15:6). It was on this group that the Holy Spirit fell on the Day of Pentecost, and Luke is careful to note that when a further three thousand accepted Peter's message they were added to the number of

6   John R. W. Stott, *The Message of Ephesians* (Leicester: Inter-Varsity Press, 1979), p. 9.

the disciples (Acts 2:41, 47. cf. Acts 5:14). Wherever the gospel was preached, whether in Samaria, Antioch, Galatia, Corinth, Ephesus, Rome or any other place covered by the apostles' missionary journeys, this pattern was repeated. The believers became *churches.*

The Greek word here is *ecclesia,* and its basic meaning is 'assembly' or 'congregation'. It was taken for granted that the converts would gather together, and very much frowned on when they didn't (Heb. 10:25). It was together that they partook of the Lord's Supper (none of them assumed that they could get on perfectly well without it), together that they were taught, together that they read the letters they received from the apostles, together that they sent out missionaries, together that they received reports from them on their return, together that they resolved such questions as the terms on which Gentiles were to be received into the church, and together that they contributed to relieving the needs of the poor. It was together that in a very special sense they enjoyed the Lord's presence, according to His own promise, 'where two or three come together in my name, there am I with them' (Matt. 18:20); and it was for the benefit of the whole body that God blessed each member with their own particular spiritual gifts (1 Cor. 12:7). They were not meant to be independent and self-sufficient spiritual units. They had been redeemed as a 'people' (Titus 2:14), mutually dependent, mutually supportive, and eager to do good together.

The early Church Fathers and the Reformers adhered steadfastly to this high view of the church. Calvin, echoing Cyprian, described the church – the *visible* church, it has to be emphasised – as the 'mother' of believers, and he developed the metaphor fully. 'There is no other way,' he declared, 'to enter into life unless this mother conceive us in her womb, give us birth, nourish us at her breast, and lastly, unless she keep us under her care and guidance until, putting off mortal flesh, we become like the angels.'[7] Only under such care can the young believer hope to grow towards spiritual adulthood and maturity (Eph. 4:11-13).

But if it is true that the church is the Christian's mother, it must be equally true that a believer without a church is a spiritual orphan. That may, of course, be forced on some by circumstances, but it is not an option any of us has a right to choose. The moving words of Ruth to Naomi are still valid today: 'Your people will be my people and your God my God' (Ruth 1:16). By its very nature, the newborn spiritual child should be crying out for its mother, and by the same token the mother should be responding to the cry: welcoming, loving, reassuring, feeding and protecting. A Christian deprived of the affection of their mother (or

---

7   John Calvin, *Institutes*, IV:I, 1. Battles edition.

depriving themselves of it) will suffer at the spiritual level the same sort of damage as a child deprived of parental affection suffers at the natural level.

This is not to say that the whole responsibility for spiritual childcare falls on ministers and elders, or on formally appointed mentors. The whole church, and every member within it, shares the responsibility, just as in a normal human family siblings and other relations quickly become involved in attending to the newborn; or, changing the metaphor, the shepherd (the pastor) feeds the sheep, and the sheep in turn feed the lambs. This was one of the most attractive features of Scottish Presbyterian polity even in the recent past. Just as in a close-knit village or township every adult was parent to every child, so in the church every mature believer was parent to every new disciple.

But the principle doesn't rest merely on the analogy of Scottish village-life. According to First Thessalonians, probably the earliest of the New Testament epistles, the Apostle Paul clearly expected the whole church to keep an eye out for those who were out of order, or timid or weak (1 Thess. 5:14); and in the same epistle he reaches out to those who have lost friends and loved ones, and reminds them that when the Lord returns the very first thing He will do will be to raise those believers who have fallen asleep; and then, turning to the whole church, he tells them: 'Comfort one another with these words' (1 Thess. 4:18, KJV).

Bereavement counselling starts at the grassroots. If we took our responsibilities seriously no Christian would ever find herself without a ministry.

One of the hallmarks of Calvinism, as we have seen, is the doctrine of the perseverance of the saints. Yet, within Calvinist churches, as within all churches, there are always some who fall away. It is easy, too easy, to take such losses in our stride, and especially to absolve ourselves by simply saying that they were never genuinely converted in the first place. But just as there is normally an element of human ministry in the conversion of sinners, is there not also an element of human ministry in the perseverance of the young convert? The spiritual post-natal care of the infant Christian is a solemn responsibility, and every casualty and fatality should trouble us greatly. Was it lack of spiritual nourishment? Was it that none acted the part of brother or sister? Or was it a hyper-Calvinism that muttered, sceptically, 'We'll see if it lasts.' Whichever, we should feel every loss keenly.

THE FREE OFFER AND PERSONAL WITNESSING

So far, our focus has been on the free offer of Christ to the unconverted, and that, of course, is a matter of paramount concern to all who have been ordained to the Christian ministry. But it is also a matter of concern to every Christian, because the duty of bearing witness to Christ devolves on every single believer, and not merely on those called to 'full-time Christian service'. Paul makes this plain when he tells the saints at Philippi that he expects them to be 'contending as one man for the faith of the gospel' (Phil. 1:27); the writer to the Hebrews makes the same point when he assumes that his readers are not only holding the faith, but professing it (Heb. 4:14); and Peter urges his readers to be prepared at all times to give an answer (an *apologia*) to anyone who asks them to give a reason for their Christian hope (1 Pet. 3:15).

It is fascinating that what Peter highlights as the key element in the Christian position (and the point on which unbelievers are most likely to challenge us) is our 'hope': a hope based on the fact that Christ has already risen (1 Pet. 1:3) and secured for us an inheritance that can 'never perish, spoil or fade' (1 Pet. 1:4). But what does he mean by being 'always prepared'? It clearly implies our knowing what our hope is and our reasons for holding it, but it also means taking care to ensure that at every moment we are in a good relationship with both God and our neighbour. It is hard to witness when we ourselves are not in a good place. But the readiness must also include the firm belief that, whoever we are talking to, God wants all people to be saved (1 Tim. 2:3-4), and our duty is to present Christ to them as a complete and faithful Saviour, to whom they are lovingly invited to come. We need to be sure of this, no matter how hopeless the spiritual condition of the person we are talking to may appear to be: sceptic, backslider, hypocrite, scoffer or debauchee. Christ is a sufficient Saviour for each, and the duty of commending Him as such follows naturally from the commandment to love our neighbour. Can we love them and yet refrain from pointing them to the way of salvation?

Yet important as it is to set Christ before our unbelieving neighbour, we also need to remember, odd though it may sound, that the free offer is not only for the unconverted. It is the only place where the soul of the troubled believer can find comfort and relief. As the Westminster Confession acknowledges (Chapter 11:5), God's children may sometimes, by their sins, fall under the displeasure of their heavenly Father, and when that happens they may find themselves in a very dark place, their sinfulness so great to their tormented eyes that forgiveness and restoration seem well-nigh impossible. How they then long for the blessedness of the one to whom God doesn't impute sin (Ps. 32:2)! Yet they know at the same time that no amendment in their own lives, and no repentance, however deep, can atone for their sins. But then, is the great word of John 6:37 not for them as surely as it is for the soul struggling with its very first conviction of sin: 'whoever comes to me I will never drive away.' Never, in any circumstances! And how precious then do those other words of John's become: 'the blood of Jesus, his Son, purifies us from all sin' (1 John 1:7). Note the phrase, 'all sin.' We grade sins on something like a scale of one-to-ten, but the moment we go down that road we are as liable to class some transgressions as 'small' as we are to class others as 'great'. The reality is that what has utterly disrupted our relationship with God is not the degree of our sin and guilt, but the fact itself, and from that standpoint all our sins are great sins. This is where we have to come back to the very heart of the gospel: the fact that on the cross of Calvary Christ bore *all* the sins of *all* His people. The troubled believer's road to recovery may be a hard one, as they 'humble themselves, confess their sins, beg pardon, and renew their faith and repentance' (Confession 11:5), but as they walk that road they are sustained by the same assurance as led them to Christ in the first place:

> Who is a pardoning God like thee?
> Or who has grace so rich and free?[8]

---

8   From the hymn, 'Great God of wonders' (Samuel Davies, 1723–61).

6

The Free Offer: Knowing Where the Fish are Hiding

The fisher of men, as Boston reminded us, has to know where the fish are hiding; or, to change the metaphor, he must know the sinner's bolt-holes and flush him out. This is no easy task. The best way to hide, of course, is to give up on church attendance altogether, and one of the tragedies of modern British society is that the vast majority of those who once received baptism never darken the door of a church. But it's not always a case of simply drifting away. Some have resolved never to go back because they genuinely fear that, if they do, they will be converted. These are not simple gospel-haters. Often they are people who, like those we read of in Hebrews 6:5, 'have tasted the goodness of the word of God' and felt themselves powerfully drawn to it, but they've seen what conversion meant for their friends, they shrink from the cost, and they resolve never to expose themselves to the same risk. Even as we preach, some may be forming that very resolution. They fear the stigma: word might get around that 'John's got religion'. They fear its impact on their careers: it might be the end of all their ambitions, especially if word gets to their employers that they've turned 'neurotic'. They may dread the thought of all the things they will need to give up, the jibe of intellectual suicide, the impact on their social lives, or all the restrictions on personal freedom which, they assume, conversion will involve.

Once they have gone, they're lost to us. We have to anticipate the danger, and a key part of this must be to clear away the misunderstandings and prejudices that surround conversion. Yes, it will mean self-denial: after all, we have to go through a narrow gate (Matt. 7:14), and that inevitably involves leaving a lot of baggage behind; but that doesn't mean that new converts have to comply with all the taboos cherished by a particular religious tradition. Instead, Christ sets us free (John 8:36), and if we are faithfully preaching the full range of Reformed theology one of the key-notes of our message will be that 'God alone is Lord of the conscience, and hath left it free from the doctrines and commandments of men' (*Westminster Confession,* 20:2). This freedom is not to be surrendered lightly. No human authority has the right to impose on young believers its own pseudo-religious conventions on leisure, sport, music, diet, dress, and political and cultural engagement. Of course, if that were the price that Christ demanded for following Him, the Christian would gladly pay it, and when the need arises he will pluck out his right eye rather than unfit himself for the service of his Saviour. But Christian discipleship can't be reduced to signing-up to a check-list of do's and don'ts. Even someone as unworldly as the late Dr Martyn Lloyd-Jones loved to listen to Mozart, watch cricket and visit agricultural shows (and that's not intended as an exhaustive list of permissible leisure-pursuits. If you prefer Bob Dylan to Mozart, then so be it. It's nobody else's business, and conversion mustn't be defined in terms of what you have to give up).

But clearing up this and similar points will hardly be enough to persuade the fugitive from 'religion' to change his mind. Nor is he or she likely to be dissuaded by arguments that demonstrate the intellectual coherence of Christianity. Many a person who has turned their back on the church does so still fully convinced that 'there is a God'. What he has to be confronted with is the greatness of this God, and with the fact that our relationship with Him is by far the most important thing in the world. He must be made to see that his response to Christ is a matter of life and death: eternal life and eternal death. His flight from Him would not matter if there were no life after death, but there is. It would not matter if Christ had not risen from the dead, but He has. It would not matter if there were neither a heaven nor a hell, but there is. The man who closes his mind against

Christ must be made to know that it is a bad bargain to win all life's glittering prizes and lose his soul. There can be no greater mistake than to assume that if, with calm deliberation, we shut Jesus Christ out of our lives we will never meet Him again. We most assuredly will.

But then, secondly, there are those who hide under the assurance, 'I am as good as any Christian.' What lies behind such a remark, clearly, is the idea that Christians view themselves as better than other people and base their hope of heaven on this very fact. But far from priding themselves on their moral superiority Christians bemoan their own spiritual poverty (Matt. 5:3). St Paul saw himself as the 'chief of sinners' (1 Tim. 1:15), and even after his conversion he called himself a 'wretched man' because he found that even when he wanted to do good, evil was right there with him (Rom. 7:21). No matter how hard he tried he repeatedly found that he fell short even of his own standards. All in all, then, when a Christian stands before God, all he can do is cry, 'God, have mercy on me, a sinner' (Luke 18:13). Our very best will not stand up to the scrutiny of the Holy One.

But we wouldn't rest with disclaiming this 'good' person's view of the way Christians think. We should venture a step further and say to him, 'Well, in that case you're ok. You don't need Christ. You already have all the goodness you require.' Still, he had better have a care. He may, indeed, be as good as any Christian; better, indeed, than any Christian, and well above the average for a human being. But that will not be the standard. The question is, Does he meet God's standard?

For example, How is it with him and the Ten Commandments? Does he love God with all his heart? Does he love his neighbour as he loves himself? And how is it between him and the Sermon on the Mount? Is he unfailingly merciful and meek? Does he never give way to lust or to anger? Does he never retaliate when injured or provoked? Does he always go the extra mile? Is he always jealous for the name of God?

Is he sure he has nothing, nothing at all, to repent of? Does his conscience never trouble him? Can he really look God in the eye and thank Him that, unlike other men, he has no need of divine mercy? Probe, probe, probe, till the man becomes a burden to himself. Only then will he begin to look for a Saviour.

Then, thirdly, there are those at the other end of the spiritual moral spectrum: people who feel that they are too bad to be saved and view themselves as beyond redemption. Sometimes this can be linked to some 'great' sin in their past or to a long and profligate career that left many broken lives in its wake. But sometimes there is no specially awful personal history, only such conviction of sin (allied to ignorance of the gospel) as leads them to think that for people like them there can be no forgiveness. Such people can be hard to reach. They are secure in their own diagnosis of their condition and no less secure in their prognosis for the future. They are gospel-proof, 'safe' behind the assurance that the good news cannot be for the likes of them.

Only God can open this lock; and yet we, too, must speak, and when we do, it is to speak *His* clear and unambiguous doctrine of justification by faith. God justifies the *ungodly* (Rom. 4:5). He doesn't demand that we atone for our own sins or earn forgiveness by great acts of penance, or cancel our guilt by performing good works; and He certainly doesn't ask that before we come pleading to Him we must first of all have renounced and conquered our sins. Instead, He extends His mercy to us just as we are; He urges us to bring our sins with us and to lay them before Him; He assures us that though we can have no claim on forgiveness, Christ has, and it's there for all who come to God in His name. Trust Him, God says, to speak for you. Trust His sacrifice to be your atonement. Trust His obedience to be your righteousness. Trust Him to break the power of sin. Trust Him to love you with a love that will never let you go. Trust Him to introduce you to His Father as His brother and as His friend. Cling to His cross. Plead His name.

This is the doctrine that the Apostle Paul set forth with such brilliant clarity in his epistles to the Romans and to the Galatians. But we also see it illustrated in some of the greatest real-life stories of the Bible. We should tell those who feel too bad to be saved the stories of men like David and Solomon and Manasseh and even St Paul himself: men who committed great sins, and yet tasted that the Lord is gracious; and tell them too of Augustine, who prayed, 'Lord, make me chaste, but not yet';[1] of John Bunyan, the compulsive swearer and blasphemer who went on to experience 'grace abounding'; and of John Newton, a brutal slave-trader till he was saved by 'amazing grace'. Above all, we must present them with that priceless word of Jesus: no one who comes will ever be turned away (John 6:37). Christ calls them, Christ invites them, Christ commands them, and they have absolutely no right to make their feelings of unworthiness an excuse for ignoring such a message, so gracious and yet so imperious. On the contrary, it is the fact that they are sinners that gives them the right to come to Christ: or, as 'Rabbi' Duncan put it, 'Sin is the handle by which I get Christ.' There was no verse in the Bible that mentions him by name and assured him, 'Christ belongs to John Duncan,' but there was a verse that assured him that 'The Son of Man is come to save that which was lost.' 'I put my finger upon that one word and say, "I'm the lost one; I'm lost."' And because he was lost, Christ belonged to him.

---

1   Augustine, *Confessions*, VIII, 17.

How perverse to reverse that argument and say, 'I'm a lost sinner, and so Christ cannot belong to me.'[2]

But, then, close by the one who is 'too bad' we meet another special case: the one who has 'let the day of grace past'. This is usually someone who has long sat under a gospel ministry and who recalls one special occasion or one particular sermon when he was so powerfully affected that he was on the verge of accepting Christ; but he didn't, and because he didn't the opportunity had passed for ever. For him there would never be a day of grace.

Preachers sometimes use stories of this kind, particularly at the close of a sermon, as a warning against refusing the gospel, and they can certainly inject an element of solemnity and drama into a gospel appeal. But such stories have no place in Christian evangelism. For anyone to say that for him the day of grace is past is to declare himself a reprobate, and that's a conclusion no one has a right to come to in this life: certainly not while he is still under the gospel, hearing God's call and His offer of mercy. Far from the day of grace being past, God is still pleading with him, and he has every right, there and then, to take God at His word and to cast himself on His grace. And just as no one has the right to consider himself a reprobate, so we have no right to think it of others, or even to plant in the mind of any of our hearers

2   A. Moody Stuart, *Recollections of the late John Duncan* (Edinburgh, Edmonston and Douglas, 1872), p. 97.

the thought that they may have let the day of grace past. Theologically, it's a meaningless concept: the 'day of grace' is God's day, not ours, and who are we to say that *He* has given up on any sinner? Only death can bring such closure; and even then, only God knows.

Nor should we ever forget that the idea of the day of grace being past can be called into service as an excuse. Yes, the story tugs at our heart-strings, but its real effect may be to provide yet another hiding-place from the gospel; a satanic shield that deflects the divine command to repent and believe. Let us not forget that many have been brought from utter despair to the joy of salvation. The preacher's commission is to instil hope, even in those who are in the pits, and through such hope to lead them to faith and repentance.

Then there are those who assume that the gospel cannot be for them because of their age, and this can be heard from both ends of the spectrum. Some will say they are too old, and perhaps accuse themselves of having misspent their lives in sin and now have no life left to offer to the Lord. But surely this should be grist to the mill of repentance, not to despair and certainly not to prolonged defiance. Old age does not exempt us from having to obey the Ten Commandments, and neither does it exempt us from the obligation to repent and believe. In any case, as far as being of no use is concerned, doesn't everyone who comes to Christ have to come saying,

'Nothing in my hand I bring'? We are driven to Him not by the ambition of being useful to Him, but by a deep sense of needing Him, and as we descend into the weaknesses and vulnerabilities of old age our need is greater than ever, and the Lord is still saying, 'Whoever comes to me will not in any circumstances be turned away.'

More commonly, however, it is the young who let the gospel pass over their heads because of their age. The very young can easily gather the impression that following Christ is a grown-up thing, and grown-ups too often confirm the impression by reacting with suspicion to signs of religion in children, especially when they apply for admission to the Lord's table. Jesus' own words are surely a sufficient rebuke to such attitudes: 'Let the little children come to me, and do not hinder them, for the kingdom of heaven belongs to such as these' (Matt. 19:14). We must never forget that some children, like John the Baptist, are born again from a very early age (and would be totally perplexed if asked to give an account of their 'conversion'). Children can develop a love for Jesus at a very early age, while all the theology they know may be contained in the words:

> Jesus loves me, this I know
> For the Bible tells me so.

But that's quite enough to enable them to put their hand in the hand of their Father in heaven as naturally as they hold the hands of their earthly mums and dads.

Yet the key point, surely, is that young people, no less than adults, *need* Jesus. They have their own sins and their own uneasy consciences and they need to know where to go for forgiveness and peace. They also have their own burdens and cares: heavier and more complex than adults realise, till they begin to think back to their own schooldays, when the world was very, very big, they were very small, and grownups could be very, very scary. They need to know that there is Someone they can bring their cares to.

But not only do young folk *need* Christ. If they have been raised in Christian homes, and especially if they have been baptised, they know that they are not their own, but that they belong to Christ and that He belongs to them. They must see everything in that light. For Him they deny themselves, and for Him they fulfil themselves, developing for Him every talent He has given them. It is always to be borne in mind, however, that Christian children are children and that their piety will be a childish piety. An early commitment to Christ should not deprive children of their childhood or prevent them sharing in the ordinary activities of children. Besides, a new adult convert, even from a distinguished professional background, is no more than a spiritual child; and a certain childishness characterises Christian believers for the whole of their lives, as the Lord Himself made plain when He declared, 'Unless you change and become like little children, you will never enter the kingdom of heaven' (Matt. 18:3). We would do better, then, to imitate little children than to censor them.

Modern evangelical churches are usually very child-aware and take great care to make them feel at home and even to feel important. Where we are failing them is in not feeding their minds. Yet, this is what they need, and this is what we are expected to deliver. We are to *instruct* our children (Eph. 6:4), and although the command is addressed to parents in the first instance it clearly involves the whole church, as Paul has already made clear by including children in his epistle (Eph. 6:1). When he himself instructs children to obey their parents he clearly assumes that he has a duty towards the church's children no less than towards its adults, and the same is surely true of the pastor/teachers who succeed him (Eph. 4:11).

This is the great need. By the time they are sixteen our children should know their way around the Bible (and shouldn't need to be told the page-number when the minister announces a text from the Book of Exodus); they should know the great stories of both the Old Testament and the New; they should know the leading doctrines of the Christian faith; they should know something of the inner meaning of the Nativity and the Crucifixion; and despite the current prejudice against rote-learning they should know the Lord's Prayer, the Ten Commandments and other biblical jewels off by heart. After all, there is no evidence that statesmen like Winston Churchill and Harold MacMillan were intellectually damaged by having memorised great reams of poetry. But they should have learned, too, that there are many things they don't know, and many things on which not all Christians are agreed; and along with that should go the humility that respects those who don't agree with them, whether Christians or non-Christians.

This is not a plea for elaborate new structures. Our immediate problem is one of attitude: a problem reflected in, for example, the trend towards dropping the name 'Sunday School' and replacing it with something like 'Junior Church'. Underlying this is the idea that young people's experience of church must be very different from their experience of school. But the fact is that the church *is* a school: the school of Christ, and in that school every Christian is a pupil, and so are their children.

Yet the educational needs of children are different from those of adults and the methods used in teaching them must differ accordingly. They can understand things, and pictures, and stories, but our sermons are full of stuff they've never seen: concepts, and principles and doctrines and the like, that mean nothing to young children. On the other hand, older children don't want childish things. This is why lessons (and they have to be lessons) have to be pitched at the right level, whether nursery, primary or secondary; this is why we need competent teachers who will bear favourable comparison with the teachers the children have in school; this is why teachers need resources; and this is why the church, and indeed every congregation, needs an educational programme which it views as central to its ministry and which it keeps under constant review. But while the instruction given in our Sunday Schools and Bible Classes should be of the very best, we should not be ashamed to admit that our overall aim is not academic. Our aim is spiritual: to present Christ to children in a manner and at a level suited to their age and level, and thus to lay a foundation on which they can build a strong, life-long discipleship. Of course, this may expose us to the charge of indoctrinating rather than educating our children, and we cannot insist too strongly that young folk must come to Christ 'most freely', or not at all. But they must know whom they believe in, and why. Only thus can they be bonded to Christ by conviction; and only thus can the church hold them by their consciences.

Yet however invaluable the instruction given in Sunday School and Bible Class, this does not absolve the pulpit of its responsibility to minister to young people, and in particular to minister to the doubts and difficulties which present such formidable obstacles to their coming to faith. From the moment they step outside the shelter of home and church they have to live in an atmosphere of unbelief; and it's not merely an atmosphere. In school, college, workplace and social life they will hear countless objections to their religion, and if the church offers no answers, the young folk will conclude that it's because we have none. This is why we have not only to preach the faith, but to defend it. Otherwise our young people will be ashamed of it. They need to hear the pulpit opening up the message of the great opening chapters of Genesis, clarifying the meaning of God's act of creation, addressing the challenge of evolution, preaching the glory of man as a bearer of the image of God, and the tragedy of man as a fallen creature. They need to hear the pulpit explain the relation between Christianity and other religions. Is there any truth in the faith of their Muslim friends? And how can we claim that Christ is the one and only way to God? More fundamentally still, how are our young people to handle the claims of their teachers and lecturers that the Bible is just another book, much of it stitched together from unknown sources, and to be treated as we would treat any other human literature?

It is irresponsible to expect Christian teenagers to deal with such issues by themselves; and for those of us in Scotland it is equally irresponsible to leave them to work out their own answers to the slurs which modern art, literature and historians cast on Calvinism and Presbyterianism, portraying them as dark, oppressive forces which for long inhibited our cultural and social development. This is a powerful ingredient in the shame which has led so many of our young people to turn their backs on the church, and the only answer in the long term is to familiarise people with the real story of Christianity in Scotland. In the meantime, however, it shouldn't be beyond our wit to introduce into the occasional sermon a tribute to the heroes of the Reformation or of the Covenant or of the Disruption, or to the many Scottish Christians, men and women, who played a pioneering role in the development of science, medicine, education, engineering and many other fields of human endeavour. Church history could easily afford better sources of illustration than pop-music and movies! But, be that as it may, what is undeniable is that if our young people lose confidence in the Bible and become ashamed of their church they will, humanly speaking, quietly slip away to places where the free offer of the gospel can never trouble them.

7

The Free Offer and the Messenger

Finally, what of the messenger? Paul's charge, 'Keep watch over yourselves,' applied in the first instance to the elders of the church in Ephesus (Acts 20:28), but it is no less relevant to their modern successors.

The first thing, surely, is that we continue to believe wholeheartedly in our own message. This may sound so elementary as to be hardly worth saying, but we must remember the inherent scepticism of the human heart with regard to the doctrines of the gospel; and we must remember, too, that all the devils of Pandemonium are united in their determination to undermine our faith. This is why one of the great comforts St Paul had as he faced the end of his life was that he had kept the faith (2 Tim. 4:7). Robert Bruce, one of the greatest preachers ever to grace a Scottish pulpit, used to remark that it was a greater matter to believe in God than people judged; and if that is true of a belief shared by all the world's religions, it is even more true of the distinctive tenets which lie at the heart of the Christian message: doctrines such as the incarnation, substitutionary atonement and Christ's resurrection from the dead.

The Church History of Scotland, and particularly of the nineteenth century, contains solemn warnings of the danger of lapsing into scepticism. Distinguished Free Church figures such as A. B. Bruce and James Denney began their ministry as brilliant champions of evangelical theology, but by the end they had departed far from it, yielding more and more ground to radical biblical criticism, and sowing the seeds of doubt on such doctrines as the deity and the sinlessness of Christ. We may be horrified to think that we could ever give up on our core Christian beliefs, but it could happen all too easily if we don't 'keep watch'; and even when we don't consciously and publicly abandon our beliefs, there may be an inner erosion of faith, the sincerity and the passion gone, and only a professional posture left. When that happens, our hearers will soon detect that the message no longer grips the preacher's heart; and on the personal level, how can we plead with others to come to Christ if we ourselves are no longer coming every hour of the day?

Amid the swirling currents of modern unbelief this is the area where, above all others, we need divine protection. Only then can we continue in our faith, established and firm, not moved from the hope held out in the gospel (Col. 1:23).

Secondly, and following on from this, the evangelist is a man who speaks with authority. The description applied in the first instance, of course, to Jesus Himself (Matt. 7:29) and it is reflected in His repeated use of the expression, 'But *I* say to you' in Matthew 5:21-48. In His case it was an inherent authority which belonged to Him as the one and only Son of God. No preacher can make such a claim. Nor can we, like the prophets, claim to have had an audience with God and emerged with a special revelation which He had charged us to deliver. Nor, yet again, can we claim that as we speak we are being carried by the Holy Spirit (2 Pet. 1:20-21) and giving *His* infallible interpretation of the will of God.

Where, then, does the source of our authority lie? It lies in Scripture, the Word of God in written form. What it says, God says, and provided we are content to be expositors of Scripture and are careful to divide it 'rightly' (2 Tim. 2:15, KJV) our messages carry the authority of God Himself. We are not preaching our own opinions or our own theories or our own 'thoughts for the day'. We are preaching what Dr Martyn Lloyd-Jones called, 'Truth unchanged, unchanging';[1] and, please God, we are preaching it, not hesitantly and diffidently, but with total certainty and confidence as *the* truth; truth which requires and commands instant belief

---

1   Dr. Martyn Lloyd-Jones, *Truth Unchanged, Unchanging* (London: James Clarke, 1951).

and instant compliance. Again, of course, the caution must be uttered that what is authoritative is the Bible properly exegeted, and we must spare no pains in seeking out its correct meaning. But once we have sought it out, we can share the confidence of men like Luther and Calvin that our preached word, derived from Scripture, is the word of God. The lessons we derive from the great narratives of Scripture, highlighting God's mighty acts, are His lessons; the doctrines we preach are His doctrines, worthy of instant credence; the promises we make, and the invitations we extend, are His promises and invitations, meriting people's wholehearted trust; the threats of which we warn are His threats, at which every man and woman should tremble; and the great moral principles we press on the human conscience, far from being the culture-bound 'points of view' of a past age, are unconditional divine imperatives which men defy at their peril, temporal and eternal. With the backing of Scripture, and fully aware that we have spoken with 'poor, lisping, stammering tongues', we can boldly declare, 'This is God's word for you today.'

Thirdly, and as hinted already, the great doctrines we preach have to be more to us than mere beliefs. They have to be our spiritual meat and drink. Before we can be preachers or evangelists we must first of all be Christians, and this means that the spiritual food we offer to others must first of all be the nourishment of our own souls. Day after day we have to trust ourselves to the eternal, wise and loyal love of God; day after day as a matter of personal urgency we have to find peace at the foot of the cross and in the doctrine of justification by faith alone; day after day we have to strive to position our hearts and our heads in heaven (Col. 3:1); day after day we have to put our own trust in the providence of God; day after day, as death removes family, friends and colleagues, we have to comfort ourselves with the knowledge that to be with Christ is far better; and day after day we have to silence our complaints with the reminder that though life may sometimes crush us we remain heirs to the unsearchable riches of Christ. The truth we preach is the truth by which we have learned to live.

Fourthly, the evangelist is a worker: a labourer. This is something the New Testament emphasises time and again. When the Lord Himself saw the fields ripe for harvest, what He asked His disciples to pray for was *labourers* (Matt. 9:38). When Paul summarised the qualifications for bishops and elders the first thing he laid down was that they should have a heart for the *task* (1 Tim. 3:1): not for status, or the prospect of a life of contemplation and prayer, but for getting the *work* done. When he gave his final instructions to Timothy, his charge was, 'Do the *work* of an evangelist' (2 Tim. 4:5). And when the Corinthians dismissed him as second-rate, he boldly replied that he had served Christ 'with far greater *labours*' (2 Cor. 11:23) than all the so-called 'super apostles', clearly implying that the hallmark of a real apostle was his willingness to toil.

The same has been true of all the great missionaries and evangelists of church history: men of the calibre of John Knox, George Whitefield, John Wesley, C. H. Spurgeon, Thomas Chalmers, William Chalmers Burns, Henry Martyn, Hudson Taylor and John MacDonald ('The Apostle of the North'). The life of each was marked by prodigious labour, and what makes this all the more remarkable is that at the same time they were men of outstanding gifts. They could easily have presumed on these gifts and got away with the minimum of toil, like the student whose trial-sermon prompted Principal Robert Rainy to remark, 'Mr So-and-So has the fatal gift of fluency': a gift which has betrayed many into a cavalier attitude to sermon-preparation, and even into taking pride in being able to preach without preparation. Preachers like Edwards and Chalmers would never have been guilty of such presumption; and neither should we. They knew that gifts could never take either the pain or the fear (1 Cor. 2:3) out of preaching; and they knew that gifts were given, not to excuse toil, but to be exercised, developed, and disciplined.

This is the point that Paul makes so vividly in 2 Timothy 1:6. Later in the epistle he will urge the younger man to endure hardship and do the *work* of an evangelist; here he tells him to 'fan into flame' the gift he has received. He is not assuming that the flame has died: Timothy clearly had his *charisma* and its flame was still burning, but it needed to be kindled and re-kindled into an ever-brighter flame. An Apollos, mighty in the Scriptures, fervent in eloquence and skilled in teaching (Acts 18:24-25), must become mightier, more eloquent and more skilled. The workman who rightly divides the word of truth (2 Tim. 2:15, KJV) must work at dividing it even more rightly. Whatever the gift we possess, whether it be knowledge, wisdom, courage, compassion, leadership, teaching or whatever else can be enlisted in the service of the gospel, we must keep developing it, acknowledging its source in God's sovereign grace, recognising its purpose as being the good of the church, fuelling it with love for God, and never forgetting that sometimes we may need an accompanying 'thorn in the flesh' to keep us humble (2 Cor. 12:7).

Some may see themselves as men of only one talent, scarcely worth fanning into flame. They should remember that it may be death to hide it (Matt. 25:30). If we have only the one, all the more reason to invest it wisely, remembering that God has sometimes achieved great things through men of limited talents such as William McCulloch of Kilsyth and Alexander MacLeod of Uig in Lewis, both of whom became instruments of memorable revivals.

On the other hand, God has entrusted some with ten talents, and He has done so only because in His view the church needed each and every one of them. This is why evangelists like Chalmers and Spurgeon laboured on so many different fronts. Chalmers, busy preacher though he was, and writing out his sermons in full, wasn't content with that. He was a prolific author, an influential theologian, a brilliant organiser, a passionate advocate of church extension and a devoted churchman. But all of it was subordinate to one great aim: the Christian good of Scotland. At the end, he was burnt-out, as were Spurgeon, Whitefield, Henry Martyn and many others, glad to spend and to be spent in the service of Christ (2 Cor. 12:15).

Yet even such men, naturally occupying positions of leadership, could sometimes find themselves weighed down with discouragement and tempted to withdraw from the field. This was probably the position of Timothy. His mentor, Paul, was about to be taken from him, and 'terrible times' were promised (2 Tim. 3:1). How could he continue? What difference could he make? But the Apostle tells him categorically, 'You are not free to abdicate. You were given a gift, and it was never more needed than it is now. Fan it into flame.'

Finally, the evangelist is a man driven by a sense of urgency. We have already seen this in that sermon of Spurgeon's with which our reflections began. Remember his rush to get down to business and the passionate intensity with which he delivered his message. This was not a man who could pursue his calling with a cool professional detachment, never breaking sweat. The evangelist is charged with delivering the greatest message the world has ever heard, and his whole heart has to be in it. It is not only a matter of physically delivering the message. Like the Virgin Mary pouring forth her soul and her spirit in the *Magnificat* (Luke 1:46-55), the evangelist will pour his heart into magnifying his Lord and rejoicing in his Saviour.

But it's not just a matter of the inherent majesty of the message. It's also a matter of the issues that hang on it. The preacher views his hearers from the standpoint of eternity, and he has to strive with might and main to persuade them to do the same; or, as David Gibson put it in his recent exposition of Ecclesiastes, he must get them to live life backwards, taking the one thing in the future that is certain (death), working back from that, and viewing all their decisions from the perspective of the end.[2] This was certainly the perspective from which Jesus taught: 'What good will it be for a man,' He asked, 'if he gains the whole world, yet forfeits his soul?' (Matt. 16:26). He faced His hearers with a choice between two ways: a narrow one, little travelled, that leads to life, and a broad one, highly popular, that leads to destruction (Matt. 7:13-14). His messenger, accordingly, will plead with men and women to choose life. Yet He will

2   David Gibson, *Living Life Backward: How Ecclesiastes Teaches us to Live in Light of the End* (Wheaton, Illinois: Crossway, 2017), p. 12.

never be content with merely pleading. He wants outcomes. He wants to turn many to righteousness. He wants to pluck men and women as brands from the burning; and though he believes with all his heart in the sovereignty of divine grace, he can never use that sovereignty as a pillow. When his appeals fail, he will weep over his unbelieving hearers because he views their unbelief from the perspective of eternity.

Without that perspective, with its issues of life and death, heaven and hell, we will never take evangelism seriously.

Appendix

Sermon by C. H. Spurgeon: Compel them to Come In (Luke 14:23)

I feel in such a haste to go out and obey this commandment this morning, by compelling those to come in who are now tarrying in the highways and hedges, that I cannot wait for an introduction, but must at once set about my business.

Hear then, O ye that are strangers to the truth as it is in Jesus – hear then the message that I have to bring you. Ye have fallen, fallen in your father Adam; ye have fallen also in yourselves, by your daily sin and your constant iniquity; you have provoked the anger of the Most High; and as assuredly as you have sinned, so certainly must God punish you if you persevere in your iniquity, for the Lord is a God of justice, and will by no means spare the guilty. But have you not heard, hath it not long been spoken in your ears, that God, in His infinite mercy, has devised a way whereby, without any infringement upon His honour, He can have mercy upon you, the guilty and the undeserving?

To you I speak; and my voice is unto you, O sons of men; Jesus Christ, very God of very God, hath descended from heaven, and was made in the likeness of sinful flesh. Begotten of the Holy Ghost, He was born of the Virgin Mary; He lived in this world a life of exemplary holiness, and of the deepest suffering, till at last He gave Himself up to die for our sins, 'the just for the unjust, to bring us to God.' And now the plan of salvation is simply declared unto you – 'Whosoever believeth in the Lord Jesus Christ shall be saved.' For you who have violated all the precepts of God, and have disdained His mercy and dared His vengeance, there is yet mercy proclaimed, for 'whosoever calleth upon the name of the Lord shall be saved'. 'For this is a faithful saying and worthy of all acceptation, that Christ Jesus came into the world to save sinners, of whom I am chief;' whosoever cometh unto Him He will in no wise cast out, for He is able also to save unto the uttermost them that come unto God by Him, seeing He ever liveth to make intercession for us.

Now all that God asks of you – and this He gives you – is that you will simply look at His bleeding dying Son, and trust your souls into the hands of Him whose name alone can save from death and hell. Is it not a marvelous thing, that the proclamation of this gospel does not receive the unanimous consent of men? One would think that as soon as ever this was preached, 'That whosoever believeth shall have eternal life,' every one of you, 'casting away every man his sins and his iniquities,' would lay hold on Jesus Christ, and look alone to His cross. But alas! such is the desperate evil of our nature, such the pernicious depravity of our character, that this message is despised, the invitation to the gospel feast is rejected, and there are many of you who are this day enemies of God by wicked works, enemies to the God who preaches Christ to you today, enemies to Him who sent His Son to give His life a ransom for many. Strange I say it is that it should be so, yet nevertheless it is the fact, and hence the necessity for the command of the text – 'Compel them to come in.'

Children of God, ye who have believed, I shall have little or nothing to say to you this morning; I am going straight to my business – I am going after those that will not come – those that are in the byways and hedges, and God going with me, it is my duty now to fulfil this command, 'Compel them to come in.'

First, I must, find you out; secondly, I will go to work to compel you to come in.

1. First, I must *Find You Out*. If you read the verses that precede the text, you will find an amplification of this command: 'Go out quickly into the streets and lanes of the city, and bring in hither the poor, the maimed, the halt, and

the blind'; and then, afterwards, 'Go out into the highways,' bring in the vagrants, the highwaymen, 'and into the hedges,' bring in those that have no resting-place for their heads, and are lying under the hedges to rest, bring them in also, and 'compel them to come in'.

Yes, I see you this morning, you that are poor. I am to compel you to come in. You are poor in circumstances, but this is no barrier to the kingdom of heaven, for God hath not exempted from His grace the man that shivers in rags, and who is destitute of bread. In fact, if there be any distinction made, the distinction is on your side, and for your benefit – 'Unto you is the word of salvation sent'; 'For the poor have the gospel preached unto them.' But especially I must speak to you who are poor, *spiritually*. You have no faith, you have no virtue, you have no good work, you have no grace, and what is poverty worse still, you have no hope. Ah, my Master has sent you a gracious invitation. Come and welcome to the marriage feast of His love. 'Whosoever will, let him come and take of the waters of life freely.' Come, I must lay hold upon you, though you be defiled with foulest filth, and though you have nought but rags upon your back, though your own righteousness has become as filthy clouts, yet must I lay hold upon you, and invite you first, and even compel you to come in.

And now I see you again. You are not only poor, but you are *maimed*. There was a time when you thought you could work out your own salvation without God's help, when you could perform good works, attend to ceremonies, and get to heaven by yourselves; but now you are maimed, the sword of the law has cut off your hands, and now you can work no longer; you say, with bitter sorrow –

> The best performance of my hands,
> Dares not appear before thy throne.

You have lost all power now to obey the law; you feel that when you would do good, evil is present with you. You are maimed; you have given up, as a forlorn hope, all attempt to save yourself, because you are maimed and your arms are gone. But you are worse off than that, for if you could not work your way to heaven, yet you could walk your way there along the road by faith; but you are maimed in the feet as well as in the hands; you feel that you cannot believe, that you cannot repent, that you cannot obey the stipulations of the gospel. You feel that you are utterly undone, powerless in every respect to do anything that can be pleasing to God. In fact, you are crying out –

> Oh, could I but believe,
> Then all would easy be,
> I would, but cannot, Lord relieve,
> My help must come from thee.

To you am I sent also. Before you am I to lift up the blood-stained banner of the cross, to you am I to preach this gospel, 'Whoso calleth upon the name of the Lord shall be saved'; and unto you am I to cry, 'Whosoever will, let him come and take of the water of life freely.'

There is yet another class. You are *halt*. You are halting between two opinions. You are sometimes seriously inclined, and at another time worldly gaiety calls you away. What little progress you do make in religion is but a limp. You have a little strength, but that is so little that you make but painful progress. Ah, limping brother, to you also is the word of this salvation sent. Though you halt between two opinions, the Master sends me to you with this message: 'How long halt ye between two opinions? if God be God, serve him; if Baal be God, serve him.' Consider thy ways; set thine house in order, for thou shalt die and not live. Because I will do this, prepare to meet thy God, O Israel! Halt no longer, but decide for God and His truth.

And yet I see another class – the *blind*. Yes, you that cannot see yourselves, that think yourselves good when you are full of evil, that put bitter for sweet and sweet for bitter, darkness for light and light for darkness; to you am I sent. You, blind souls that cannot see your lost estate, that do not believe that sin is so exceedingly sinful as it is, and who will not be persuaded to think that God is a just and righteous God, to you am I sent. To you too that cannot see the Saviour, that see no beauty in Him that you should desire Him; who see no excellence in virtue, no glories in religion, no happiness in serving God, no delight in being His children; to you, also, am I sent.

Ay, to whom am I not sent if I take my text? For it goes further than this – it not only gives a particular description, so that each individual case may be met, but afterwards it makes a general sweep, and says, 'Go into the highways and hedges.' Here we bring in all ranks and conditions of men – my lord upon his horse in the highway, and the woman trudging about her business, the thief waylaying the traveller – all these are in the highway, and they are all to be compelled to come in, and there away in the hedges there lie some poor souls whose refuges of lies are swept away, and who are seeking not to find some little shelter for their weary heads, to you, also, are we sent this morning. This is the universal command – compel them to come in.

Now, I pause after having described the character, I pause to look at the herculean labour that lies before me. Well did Melanchthon say, 'Old Adam was too strong for young Melanchthon.' As well might a little child seek to compel a Samson, as I seek to lead a sinner to the cross of Christ. And yet my Master sends me about the errand. Lo, I see the great mountain before me of human depravity and stolid indifference, but by faith I cry, 'Who art thou, O great mountain? before Zerubbabel thou shalt become a plain.'

Does my Master say, compel them to come in? Then, though the sinner be like Samson and I a child, I shall lead him with a thread. If God saith *do* it, if I attempt it in faith *it shall be done*; and if with a groaning, struggling, and weeping heart, I so seek this day to compel sinners to come to Christ, the sweet compulsions of the Holy Spirit shall go with every word, and some indeed shall be compelled to come in.

2. And now to the work – directly to the work. Unconverted, unreconciled, unregenerate men and women, I am to *Compel You to Come In*. Permit me first of all to accost you in the highways of sin and tell you over again my errand. The King of heaven this morning sends a gracious invitation to you. He says, 'As I live, saith the Lord, I have no pleasure in the death of him that dieth, but had rather that he should turn unto me and live'; 'Come now, and let us reason together, saith the Lord, though your sins be as scarlet they shall be as wool; though they be red like crimson they shall be whiter than snow.' Dear brother, it makes my heart rejoice to think that I should have such good news to tell you, and yet I confess my soul is heavy because I see you do not think it good news, but turn away from it, and do not give it due regard. Permit me to tell you what the King has done for you. He knew your guilt, He foresaw that you would ruin yourself. He knew that His justice would demand your blood, and in order that this difficulty might be escaped,

that His justice might have its full due, and that you might yet be saved, *Jesus Christ hath died*.

Will you just for a moment glance at this picture? You see that man there on his knees in the garden of Gethsemane, sweating drops of blood. You see this next: you see that miserable sufferer tied to a pillar and lashed with terrible scourges, till the shoulder bones are seen like white islands in the midst of a sea of blood. Again you see this third picture; it is the same man hanging on the cross with hands extended, and with feet nailed fast, dying, groaning, bleeding; methought the picture spoke and said, 'It is finished.' Now all this hath Jesus Christ of Nazareth done, in order that God might consistently with His justice pardon sin; and the message to you this morning is this – 'Believe on the Lord Jesus Christ and thou shalt be saved.' That is, trust Him, renounce thy works, and thy ways, and set thine heart alone on this man, who gave Himself for sinners.

Well brother, I have told you the message, what sayest thou unto it? Do you turn away? You tell me it is nothing to you; you cannot listen to it; that you will hear me by-and-by; but you will go your way this day and attend to your farm and merchandise. Stop brother, I was not told merely to tell you and then go about my business. No; I am told to compel you to come in; and permit me to observe to you before I further go, that there is one thing I can say – and to which God is my witness this morning, that I am in earnest with you in my desire that you should comply with this command of God. You may despise your own salvation, but I do not despise it; you may go away and forget what you shall hear, but you will please to remember that the things I now say cost me many a groan ere I came here to utter them. My inmost soul is speaking out to you, my poor brother, when I beseech you by him that liveth and was dead, and is alive for evermore, consider my master's message which He bids me now address to you.

But do you spurn it? Do you still refuse it? Then I must change my tone a minute. I will not merely tell you the message, and invite you as I do with all earnestness, and sincere affection – I will go further. Sinner, in God's name I *command* you to repent and believe. Do you ask me whence my authority? I am an ambassador of heaven. My credentials, some of them secret, and in my own heart; and others of them open before you this day in the seals of my ministry, sitting and standing in this hall, where God has given me many souls for my hire.

As God the everlasting one hath given me a commission to preach His gospel, I command you to believe in the Lord Jesus Christ; not on my own authority, but on the authority of Him who said, 'Go ye into all the world and preach the gospel to every creature'; and then annexed this solemn sanction, 'He that believeth and is baptized shall be saved, but he that believeth not shall be damned.' Reject my message, and remember 'He that despised Moses' law, died without mercy under two or three witnesses: of how much sorer punishment, suppose ye, shall he be thought worthy, who hath trodden under foot the Son of God.' An ambassador is not to stand below the man with whom he deals, for we stand higher. If the minister chooses to take his proper rank, girded with the omnipotence of God, and anointed with his holy unction, he is to command men, and speak with all authority compelling them to come in: 'command, exhort, rebuke with all long-suffering.'

But do you turn away and say you will not be commanded? Then again will I change my note. If that avails not, all other means shall be tried. My brother, I come to you simple of speech, and I exhort you to flee to Christ. O my brother, dost thou know what a loving Christ He is? Let me tell thee from my own soul what I know of Him. I, too, once despised Him. He knocked at the door of my heart and I refused to open it. He came to me, times without number, morning by morning, and night by night; He checked me in my conscience and spoke to me by His Spirit, and when, at last, the thunders of the law prevailed in my conscience, I thought that Christ was cruel and unkind. O I can never forgive myself that I should have thought so ill of Him. But what a loving reception did I have when I went to Him. I thought He would smite me, but His hand was not clenched in anger but opened wide in mercy. I thought full sure that

His eyes would dart lightning-flashes of wrath upon me; but, instead thereof, they were full of tears. He fell upon my neck and kissed me; He took off my rags and did clothe me with His righteousness, and caused my soul to sing aloud for joy; while in the house of my heart and in the house of His church there was music and dancing, because His son that He had lost was found, and He that was dead was made alive. I exhort you, then, to look to Jesus Christ and to be lightened. Sinner, you will never regret – I will be bondsman for my Master that you will never regret it – you will have no sigh to go back to your state of condemnation; you shall go out of Egypt and shall go into the promised land and shall find it flowing with milk and honey. The trials of Christian life you shall find heavy, but you will find grace will make them light. And as for the joys and delights of being a child of God, if I lie this day you shall charge me with it in days to come. If you will taste and see that the Lord is good, I am not afraid but that you shall find that He is not only good, but better than human lips ever can describe.

I know not what arguments to use with you. I appeal to your own self-interests. Oh my poor friend, would it not be better for you to be reconciled to the God of heaven, than to be His enemy? What are you getting by opposing God? Are you the happier for being His enemy? Answer, pleasure-seeker; hast thou found delights in that cup? Answer me, self-righteous man: hast thou found rest for the sole of thy foot in all thy works? Oh thou that goest about to establish thine own righteousness, I charge thee let conscience speak. Hast thou found it to be a happy path? Ah, my friend, 'Wherefore dost thou spend thy money for that which is not bread, and thy labour for that which satisfieth not; hearken diligently unto me, and eat ye that which is good, and let your soul delight itself in fatness.' I exhort you by everything that is sacred and solemn, everything that is important and eternal, flee for your lives, look not behind you, stay not in all the plain, stay not until you have proved, and found an interest in the blood of Jesus Christ, that blood which cleanseth us from all sin.

Are you still cold and indifferent? Will not the blind man permit me to lead him to the feast? Will not my maimed brother put his hand upon my shoulder and permit me to assist him to the banquet? Will not the poor man allow me to walk side-by-side with him? Must I use some stronger words. Must I use some other compulsion to compel you to come in?

Sinners, this one thing I am resolved upon this morning, if you be not saved ye shall be without excuse. Ye, from the grey-headed down to the tender age of childhood, if ye this day lay not hold on Christ, your blood shall be on your own head. If there be power in man to bring his fellow, (as there is when man is helped by the Holy Spirit) that power shall be exercised this morning, God helping me. Come, I am not to be put off by your rebuffs; if my exhortation fails, I must come to something else. My brother, I entreat you, I entreat you stop and consider. Do you know what it is you are rejecting this morning? You are rejecting Christ, your only Saviour. 'Other foundation can no man lay;' 'there is none other name given among men whereby we must be saved.'

My brother, I cannot bear that ye should do this, for I remember what you are forgetting: the day is coming when you will want a Saviour. It is not long ere weary months shall have ended, and your strength begin to decline; your pulse shall fail you, your strength shall depart, and you and the grim monster – death – must face each other. What will you do in the swellings of Jordan without a Saviour? Death-beds are stony things without the Lord Jesus Christ. It is an awful thing to die anyhow; he that hath the best hope, and the most triumphant faith, finds that death is not a thing to laugh at. It is a terrible thing to pass from the seen to the unseen, from the mortal to the immortal, from time to eternity, and you will find it hard to go through the iron gates of death without the sweet wings of angels to conduct you to the portals of the skies. It will be a hard thing to die without Christ. I cannot help thinking of you. I see you acting the suicide this morning, and I picture myself standing at your bedside and hearing your cries, and knowing that you are dying without hope. I cannot bear that. I think I am standing by your coffin now, and looking into your clay-cold face, and saying. 'This man despised Christ and neglected the great salvation.' I think what bitter tears I shall weep then, if I think that I have been unfaithful to you, and how those eyes fast closed in death, shall seem to chide me and say, 'Minister, I attended the music hall, but you were not in earnest with me; you amused me, you preached to me, but you did not plead with me. You did not know what Paul meant when he said, "As though God did beseech you by us we pray you in Christ's stead, be ye reconciled to God."'

I entreat you let this message enter your heart for another reason. I picture myself standing at the bar of God. As the Lord liveth, the day of judgment is coming. You believe that? You are not an infidel; your conscience would not permit you to doubt the Scripture. Perhaps you may have pretended to do so, but you cannot. You feel there must be a day when God shall judge the world in righteousness. I see you standing in the midst of that throng, and the eye of God is fixed on you. It seems to you that He is not looking anywhere else, but only upon you, and He summons you before Him; and He reads your sins, and He cries, 'Depart, ye cursed, into everlasting fire in hell!' My hearer, I cannot bear to think of you in that position; it seems as if every hair on my head must stand on end to think of any hearer of mine being damned. Will you picture yourselves in that position? The word has gone forth, 'Depart, ye cursed.' Do you see the pit as it opens to swallow you up? Do you listen to the shrieks and the yells of those who have preceded you to that eternal lake of torment?

Instead of picturing the scene, I turn to you with the words of the inspired prophet, and I say, 'Who among us shall dwell with the devouring fire? Who among us shall dwell with everlasting burnings?' Oh! my brother, I cannot let you put away religion thus; no, I think of what is to come after death. I should be destitute of all humanity if I should see a person about to poison himself, and did not dash away the cup; or if I saw another about to plunge from London Bridge, if I did not assist in preventing him from doing so; and I should be worse than a fiend if I did not now, with all love, and kindness, and earnestness, beseech you to 'lay hold on eternal life', 'to labour not for the meat that perisheth, but for the meat that endureth unto everlasting life.'

Some hyper-calvinist would tell me I am wrong in so doing. I cannot help it. I must do it. As I must stand before my Judge at last, I feel that I shall not make full proof of my ministry unless I entreat with many tears that ye would be saved, that ye would look unto Jesus Christ and receive His glorious salvation. But does not this avail? are all our entreaties lost upon you; do you turn a deaf ear? Then again I change my note. Sinner, I have pleaded with you as a man pleadeth with his friend, and were it for my own life

I could not speak more earnestly this morning than I do speak concerning yours. I did feel earnest about my own soul, but not a whit more than I do about the souls of my congregation this morning; and therefore, if ye put away these entreaties I have something else – I must threaten you. You shall not always have such warnings as these. A day is coming, when hushed shall be the voice of every gospel minister, at least for you; for your ear shall be cold in death. It shall not be any more threatening; it shall be the fulfillment of the threatening. There shall be no promise, no proclamations of pardon and of mercy; no peace-speaking blood, but you shall be in the land where the Sabbath is all swallowed up in everlasting nights of misery, and where the preachings of the gospel are forbidden because they would be unavailing.

I charge you then, listen to this voice that now addresses your conscience; for if not, God shall speak to you in His wrath, and say unto you in His hot displeasure, 'I called and ye refused; I stretched out my hand and no man regarded; therefore will I mock at your calamity; I will laugh when your fear cometh.' Sinner, I threaten you again. Remember, it is but a short time you may have to hear these warnings. You imagine that your life will be long, but do you know how short it is? Have you ever tried to think how frail you are? Did you ever see a body when it has been cut in pieces by the anatomist? Did you ever see such a marvellous thing as the human frame?

> Strange, a harp of a thousand strings,
> Should keep in tune so long.

Let but one of those cords be twisted, let but a mouthful of food go in the wrong direction, and you may die. The slightest chance, as we have it, may send you swift to death, when God wills it. Strong men have been killed by the smallest and slightest accident, and so may you. In the chapel, in the house of God, men have dropped down dead. How often do we hear of men falling in our streets – rolling out of time into eternity, by some sudden stroke. And are you sure that heart of yours is quite sound? Is the blood circulating with all accuracy? Are you quite sure of that? And if it be so, how long shall it be? O, perhaps there are some of you here that shall never see Christmas Day; it may be the mandate has gone forth already, 'Set thine house in order, for thou shalt die and not live.' Out of this vast congregation, I might with accuracy tell how many will be dead in a year; but certain it is that the whole of us shall never meet together again in any one assembly. Some out of this vast crowd, perhaps some two or three, shall depart ere the new year shall be ushered in.

I remind you, then, my brother, that either the gate of salvation may be shut, or else you may be out of the place where the gate of mercy stands. Come, then, let the threatening have power with you. I do not threaten because I would alarm without cause, but in hopes that a brother's threatening may drive you to the place where God hath prepared the feast of the gospel. And now, *must I turn hopelessly away?* Have I exhausted all that I can say? No, I will come to you again. Tell me what it is, my brother, that keeps you from Christ.

I hear one say, 'Oh, sir, it is because I feel myself too guilty.' That cannot be, my friend, that cannot be. 'But, sir, I am the chief of sinners.' Friend, you are not. The chief of sinners died and went to heaven many years ago; his name was Saul of Tarsus, afterwards called Paul the Apostle. He was the chief of sinners, I know he spoke the truth. 'No,' but you say still, 'I am too vile.' You cannot be viler than the chief of sinners. You must, at least, be second worst. Even supposing you are the worst now alive, you are second worst, for he was chief. But suppose you are the worst, is not that the very reason why you should come to Christ? The worse a man is, the more reason he should go to the hospital or physician. The more poor you are, the more reason you should accept the charity of another. Now, Christ does not want any merits of yours. He gives freely. The worse you are, the more welcome you are. But let me ask you a question: Do you think you will ever get better by stopping away from Christ? If so, you know very little as yet of the way of salvation at all. No, sir, the longer you stay, the worse you will grow; your hope will grow weaker, your despair will become stronger; the nail with which Satan has fastened you down will be more firmly clenched, and you will be less hopeful than ever. Come, I beseech you, recollect there is nothing to be gained by delay, but by delay everything may be lost.

'But,' cries another, 'I feel I cannot believe.' No, my friend, and you never will believe if you look first at your believing. Remember, I am not come to invite you to faith, but am come to invite you to Christ. But you say, 'What is the difference?' Why, just this, if you first of all say, 'I want to believe a thing,' you never do it. But your first inquiry must be, 'What is this thing that I am to believe?' Then will faith come as the consequence of that search. Our first business has not to do with faith, but with Christ. Come, I beseech you, on Calvary's mount, and see the cross. Behold the Son of God, He who made the heavens and the earth, dying for your sins. Look to Him, is there not power in Him to save? Look at His face so full of pity. Is there not love in His heart to prove him *willing* to save? Sure sinner, the sight of Christ will help thee to believe. Do not believe first, and then go to Christ, or else thy faith will be a worthless thing; go to Christ without any faith, and cast thyself upon Him, sink or swim.

But I hear another cry, 'Oh sir, you do not know how often I have been invited, how long I have rejected the Lord.' I do not know, and I do not want to know; all I know is that my Master has sent me to compel you to come in; so come along with you now. You may have rejected a thousand invitations; don't make this the thousandth-and-one. You have been up to the house of God, and you have only been gospel hardened. But do I not see a tear in your eye; come, my brother, don't be hardened by this morning's sermon. O, Spirit of the living God, come and melt this heart for it has never been melted, and compel him to come in! I cannot let you go on such idle excuses as that; if you have lived so many years slighting Christ, there are so many reasons why now you should not slight Him. But did I hear you whisper that this was not a convenient time? Then what must I say to you? When will that convenient time come? Shall it come when you are in hell? Will that time be convenient? Shall it come when you are on your dying bed, and the death throttle is in your throat – shall it come then? Or when the burning sweat is scalding your brow; and then again, when the cold clammy sweat is there, shall those be convenient times? When pains are racking you, and you are on the borders of the tomb? No, sir, this morning is the convenient time. May God make it so.

Remember, I have no authority to ask you to come to Christ tomorrow. The Master has given you no invitation to come to him next Tuesday. The invitation is, '*Today* if ye will hear His voice, harden not your hearts as in the provocation,' for the Spirit saith 'today'. 'Come *now* and let us reason together;' why should you put it off? It may be the last warning you shall ever have. Put it off, and you may never weep again in chapel. You may never have so earnest a discourse addressed to you. You may not be pleaded with as I would plead with you now. You may go away, and God may say, 'He is given unto idols, let him alone.' He shall throw the reins upon your neck; and then, mark – your course is sure, but it is sure damnation and swift destruction.

And now again, is it all in vain? Will you not now come to Christ? Then what more can I do? I have but one more resort, and that shall be tried. I can be permitted to weep for you; I can be allowed to pray for you. You shall scorn the address if you like; you shall laugh at the preacher; you shall call him fanatic if you will; he will not chide you, he will bring no accusation against you to the great Judge. Your offence, so far as he is concerned, is forgiven before it is committed; but you will remember that the message that you are rejecting this morning is a message from one who loves you, and it is given to you also by the lips of one who loves you. You will recollect that you may play your soul away with the devil, that you may listlessly think it a matter of no importance; but there lives at least one who is in earnest about your soul, and one who before he came here wrestled with his God for strength to preach to you, and who when he has gone from this place will not forget his hearers of this morning. I say again, when words fail us we can give tears – for words and tears are the arms with which gospel ministers compel men to come in.

You do not know, and I suppose could not believe, how anxious a man whom God has called to the ministry feels about his congregation, and especially about some of them. I heard but the other day of a young man who attended here a long time, and his father's hope was that he would be brought to Christ. He became acquainted, however, with an infidel; and now he neglects his business, and lives in a daily course of sin. I saw his father's poor wan face; I did not ask him to tell me the story himself, for I felt it was raking up a trouble and opening a sore; I fear, sometimes, that good man's grey hairs may be brought with sorrow to the grave. Young men, you do not pray for yourselves, but your mothers wrestle for you. You will not think of your own souls, but your father's anxiety is exercised for you. I have been at prayer meetings, when I have heard children of God pray there, and they could not have prayed with more earnestness and more intensity of anguish if they had been each of them seeking their own soul's salvation. And is it not strange that we should be ready to move heaven and earth for your salvation, and that still you should have no thought for yourselves, no regard to eternal things?

Now I turn for one moment to some here. There are some of you here members of Christian churches, who make a profession of religion, but unless I be mistaken in you – and I shall be happy if I am – your profession is a lie. You do not live up to it, you dishonour it; you can live in the perpetual practice of absenting yourselves from God's house, if not in sins worse than that. Now I ask such of you who do not adorn the doctrine of God your Saviour, do you imagine that you can call me your pastor, and yet that my soul cannot tremble over you and in secret weep for you? Again, I say it may be but little concern to you how you defile the garments of your Christianity, but it is a great concern to God's hidden ones, who sigh and cry, and groan for the iniquities of the professors of Zion.

Now does anything else remain to the minister besides weeping and prayer? Yes, there is one thing else. God has given to His servants not the power of regeneration, but He has given them something akin to it. It is impossible for any man to regenerate his neighbour; and yet how are men born to God? Does not the Apostle say of such a one that he was begotten by him in his bonds? Now the minister has a power given him of God, to be considered both the father and the mother of those born to God, for the Apostle said he travailed in birth for souls till Christ was formed in them. What can we do then? We can now appeal to the Spirit. I know I have preached the gospel, that I have preached it earnestly; I challenge my Master to honour His own promise. He has said it shall not return unto me void, and it shall not. It is in His hands, not mine. I cannot compel you, but thou O Spirit of God who hast the key of the heart, thou canst compel. Did you ever notice in that chapter of the Revelation, where it says, 'Behold I stand at the door and knock,' a few verses before, the same person is described, as he who hath the key of David. So that if knocking will not avail, he has the key and can and will come in. Now if the knocking of an earnest minister prevail not with you this morning, there remains still that secret opening of the heart by the Spirit, so that you shall be compelled.

I thought it my duty to labour with you as though I must do it; now I throw it into my Master's hands. It cannot be His will that we should travail in birth, and yet not bring forth spiritual children. It is with Him; he is master of the heart, and the day shall declare it, that some of you constrained by sovereign grace have become the willing captives of the all-conquering Jesus, and have bowed your hearts to Him through the sermon of this morning.

SHARED
LIFE

THE TRINITY & THE FELLOWSHIP OF GOD'S PEOPLE

DONALD MACLEOD

Shared Life

The Trinity and the Fellowship of God's People

Donald Macleod

What is the trinity and does it really matter? Donald Macleod tells us that it does matter as 'it is the model for the way we should live, particularly in our relations with one another.' The Bible teaches clearly about the relationship between Father, Son and Holy Spirit. Fully grasping the trinity will always be beyond us, after all it is a divine mystery, but we can understand it better and it is critically important that we do, for if our understanding of God is wrong, it follows that our other ideas may be wrong too. 'The doctrine of the Trinity is not simply something to be believed, but something that ought to affect our lives profoundly', says Donald Macleod in this useful book that teaches us about the concept and implications of the doctrine of the Trinity.

...gives us a helpful look at the objections raised by Judaism, Islam, Mormonism and the Jehovah's Witnesses... extremely helpful. Donald Macleod writes with his customary clarity.

Evangelism Today

978-1-8579-2128-1

Donald
Macleod

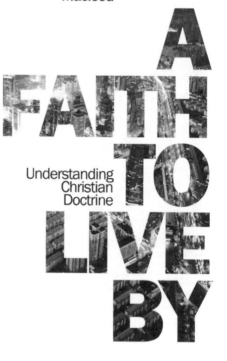

Understanding
Christian
Doctrine

A Faith to Live By

Understanding Christian Doctrine

Donald Macleod

This is a comprehensive examination of Christian doctrine, practically explained – The Inspiration of Scripture, the Trinity, Sin, the Incarnation, the Atonement, Justification, Christian Liberty, Baptism, the Church, the Lord's Supper, the Second Coming, the Resurrection, Hell and Heaven. It equips the reader to present their faith intelligently to others.

… a master of making difficult things seem simple, without compromising their profundity … Macleod is simultaneously an able apologist and a world class exegete … Learn from Macleod. Argue with Macleod. And then bow the knee to your Saviour, the Lord Jesus Christ, and worship.

Ligon Duncan
Chancellor and CEO, Reformed Theological Seminary

978-1-8455-0585-1

Christian Focus Publications

Our mission statement –

STAYING FAITHFUL

In dependence upon God we seek to impact the world through literature faithful to His infallible Word, the Bible. Our aim is to ensure that the Lord Jesus Christ is presented as the only hope to obtain forgiveness of sin, live a useful life and look forward to heaven with Him.

Our books are published in four imprints:

CHRISTIAN
FOCUS

Popular works including biographies, commentaries, basic doctrine and Christian living.

CHRISTIAN
HERITAGE

Books representing some of the best material from the rich heritage of the church.

MENTOR

Books written at a level suitable for Bible College and seminary students, pastors, and other serious readers. The imprint includes commentaries, doctrinal studies, examination of current issues and church history.

CF4·K

Children's books for quality Bible teaching and for all age groups: Sunday school curriculum, puzzle and activity books; personal and family devotional titles, biographies and inspirational stories – because you are never too young to know Jesus!

Christian Focus Publications Ltd,
Geanies House, Fearn, Ross-shire,
IV20 1TW, Scotland, United Kingdom.
www.christianfocus.com